W. ROYCE ADAMS
Santa Barbara City College

FOR BETTER
READING

Holt, Rinehart and Winston

New York   Chicago   San Francisco   Atlanta   Dallas   Montreal   Toronto

Library of Congress Cataloging in Publication Data

Adams, W. Royce.
  PREP: for better reading.
    1. Reading—Remedial teaching.   2. Readers.
3. Vocabulary.   I. Title.
LB1050.5.A325   428'.4'0711   79–16416
ISBN 0–03–047011–0

PREFACE

PREP: For Better Reading is designed for college students experiencing difficulties with their reading skills. This text is the culmination of the following blends: one, the results of a questionnaire sent to over two thousand reading instructors, asking what they would like to see in a reading textbook of a remedial nature primarily for two-year college students, adult basic education students, and advanced ESL (English as a Second Language) students; two, current available research and recorded methodology on teaching secondary and college reading; and, three, the author's twenty years of experience teaching reading at the secondary and college levels. The advantage is a tightly structured, eclectic reading skills text that provides students who need additional help an opportunity to develop the basic reading skills they lack.

The book contains three units consisting of three chapters each. At the end of each unit there is a Unit Check Test based on the content of each unit's three chapters. Each chapter has a list of its objectives at the beginning. Chapters are divided into four parts: **P.R.E.P.** "**P:** Pre-reading Drills" presents a selected vocabulary list, plus word usage and visual discrimination drills based on words from the reading selection in the chapter. "**R:** Reading Drill" presents a reading selection using a modified Directed Reading-Thinking Activity (DRTA) method. A tear-out comprehension check follows each selection for submission to the instructor. Using the Fry Readability Formula, reading selections range from fourth to eighth grade levels progressively. "**E:** Exercises in Vocabulary" presents word attack skills of all types and word knowledge skills in a variety of drills from phonics to Greek and Latin word parts. Again, a vocabulary check tear-out sheet is provided for the instructor's use. "**P:** Perfecting Reading Skills" provides practice in everything from comprehending short phrases to interpreting maps, tables, and graphs. Though comprehension questions are not labeled as such, skills covered include recognizing main ideas, sequence of events, cause-effect rela-

tionships, drawing inferences, following directions, organizing information, and author's bias. Answers to most drills appear in the text for individual lab and classroom use. Answers to important check tests and
unit tests appear in the *Instructor's Manual*. Charts for recording test
results appear in the back of the text.

The *Instructor's Manual* provides the rationale for the design and the
use of certain types of drills in the text. It also offers some suggested
readings from books and journals for instructors who wish to improve
their own knowledge of teaching reading skills at the college level, and
it also gives some suggestions for using the text as well as the answers
to check tests. The manual may be obtained through a local Holt repre-
sentative or by writing to the English Editor, College Department, Holt,
Rinehart and Winston, 383 Madison Avenue, New York, NY 10017.

PREP can be used in a classroom situation or in an individualized
reading program. There is much self-directed student activity involve-
ment; however, students needing the reading skills provided here
should receive constant follow-up and reinforcement through tutorial
or small-group discussion and instruction.

Appreciation is given to all those who answered the questionnaires
sent by the publisher. The following reviewers provided helpful suggestions: Rhoda Lintz Casey, Compton Community College; D. W. Cum-
mings, Central Washington University; Lee Kolzow, William Rainey
Harper College; Cheryl McKernan, Central Washington University,
Barbara G. Reale, Aims Community College; and Suzanne Stevens,
Skyline College. For their editorial expertise, I wish to thank Kenney
Withers, Susan Katz, and Lester A. Sheinis of Holt, Rinehart and Winston.

W.R.A.

Contents

CHAPTER 9 268

PREP TALK: WHAT IT TAKES TO CATCH UP

Let's be straight. Chances are you are a college freshman. But chances are you don't have a terrific high school grade record. You're probably not too sure why you're in college except that you've been told it's good for you and you'll get a better job if you go to college. You probably are not used to reading or studying much. Perhaps you haven't been in school for a while and you're a little nervous. Maybe you even have a bad self-image. Maybe you've already taken reading courses and don't feel that they have done you much good. And maybe you don't feel too hot about taking a reading course when you're in college because you know you should have the skills this course teaches.

Well, forget all that. It's all past stuff. Now you have a chance to catch up. Working in this book can bring your reading scores and skills closer to college level. The drills you need are here. What's needed now is for *you* to be here—really here wanting to learn. Get off your case, and give yourself a chance to learn what you missed somewhere, whatever the reasons. Now you have a chance to do what you didn't or couldn't do before. Don't waste any more time. Give this book and this course all you've got. It's probably more important than any other class you're taking right now.

As you work through this book, don't be afraid to ask questions. No question is dumb if you don't know the answer. Don't worry about mistakes you may make. Learn from them.

Take this book, this course, and yourself seriously. You *can* learn to read better.

UNIT 1

CHAPTER 1

Objectives

P: PREREADING DRILLS

A. Words to Know
B. Warm-up Drills

R: READING DRILL

A. Reading and Thinking About What You Read
"Stevie Wonder: Sunshine in the Shadow" by Linda Jacobs
B. Comprehension Check

E: EXERCISES IN VOCABULARY

A. Drills
1: Part A, The Alphabet
2: Part B, Expanding Words
2: Consonant Blends
3: Vowel Sounds Review
4: Double Vowels Review
5: Words That Sound Alike
B. Vocabulary Check

P: PERFECTING READING SKILLS

A. Comprehending Phrases
B. Comprehending Sentences
C. Comprehending This Chapter

OBJECTIVES

When you are finished working in this chapter, you will

1. Recognize and be able to use at least 90 percent of the vocabulary words presented in the "Words to Know" section.

2. Have started to develop your ability to recognize words faster.

3. Know what vowels are and their basic sounds.

4. Know what consonants are and what consonant blends and digraphs are.

5. Know what homonyms are and be able to name at least ten homonyms.

6. Have developed your comprehension of phrases and sentences by noting how key words and phrases are used in sentences to give the main idea.

7. Have experienced answering comprehension questions that help develop your ability to recall, interpret, and apply what you have read.

P: PREREADING DRILLS

A. Words to Know

Directions. Here are some words that appear in the drills and article you will be reading in this chapter. Read them aloud, and learn the definitions of the ones you don't know.

1. *romp*—to play or play freely and in a lively manner.

   Stevie liked to romp around in the backyard with his dog.

2. *wail*—a sad, high-toned cry.

   The dog let out a wail when the girl stepped on its tail.

3. *whack*—a sharp slap.

   The girl's mother gave the girl a whack for hurting the dog.

4. *frustration*—feeling of not being able to do what you want.

   We felt Dad's frustration when the TV went out just before the end of the game.

5. *shinnied* (past tense of *to shinny*)—climbed by using hands and legs.
   Pablo shinnied up the pole.

6. *hijinks*—pranks, jokes.

   Uncle Ed's hijinks are not always funny.

7. *audition*—a testing or hearing, as when a musician or an actor tries out.

   George wants an audition so that he can try out for the play.

8. *decade*—ten years.

   Two decades add up to twenty years.

9. *flurry*—sudden movement; unexpected quickness.

   Ali threw a flurry of punches at Leon.

10. *professional*—a person whose job requires advanced study or one who earns money from sports.

    Muhammad Ali is the greatest professional boxer of all time.

B. Warm-up Drills

Drill 1

Directions. Some words are often misread because they are read too quickly. Read each sentence below, and look carefully at the two words under it. Then write in the correct word in the blank.

1. That was _____ a blow.

   quit   quite

2. When he saw Sue his _____ was to call out.

   thought   though

3. The cans fell with a _____.

   cash   clash

4. The snow _____ came out of nowhere.

   furry   flurry

5. The _____ loved his singing.

   audience   audition

6. Stevie _____ himself to play the harmonica and the piano.

   thought   taught

7. When Ira's _____ came up for renewal, he refused to sign.

   contact   contract

8. They had _____ control over him.

   compete   complete

Check your answers and your spelling with these: 1. quite, 2. thought, 3. clash, 4. flurry, 5. audience, 6. taught, 7. contract, 8. complete.

Drill 2

Directions. Move your eyes rapidly across each line. Mark the word by the number each time it appears on the same line. For example:

1. laugh   tough   ~~laugh~~   tough   ~~laugh~~   tough
2. right   night   night   ~~right~~   ~~right~~   night

Don't look back on any line. If you make a mistake, don't stop to change your answer. Keep moving on. Try to finish in less than forty seconds. Begin timing.

1. rear   rear   roar   rear   roar   roar
2. reared   roared   reared   roared   roared   reared
3. bear   bare   bear   bare   bear   bare
4. pound   pound   round   round   pound   round
5. romp   rump   rump   romp   rump   rump
6. plates   pleats   pleats   pleats   plates   plates
7. shed   shred   shed   shed   shred   shred
8. fume   fumed   fumed   fume   fumed   fumed
9. smash   smart   smash   smart   smash   smart
10. quiet   quit   quite   quiet   quit   quite
11. pride   pride   prod   prank   pride   print
12. clash   clamp   clump   clamp   clash   clash
13. wailed   walled   wailed   walled   wailed   wails
14. formula   formulate   formula   familiar   formula   former
15. decade   decayed   decay   decade   decade   decade

TIME: _____

Now check each line to see if you marked the correct word every time it appears. Make sure you can pronounce all the words. Learn definitions of words you don't know by discussing them in class. The words by the numbers all appear in the article you are going to read in this chapter.

TOTAL LINES CORRECT: _____

Drill 3

Directions. Follow the same directions as Drill 2. Remember, work quickly. Don't look back on a line. Don't change any mistakes you may make. Try to finish in less than forty seconds.
Begin timing.

1. faintly	faint faints faintly frankly faintly
2. poverty	poverty probably poverty proven poverty
3. granted	grants grant granted grandly grant
4. whack	whacked whopped whacky whack whack
5. frustrates	frustration frustrate frustrates fluster
6. fussed	fussy fuss fussily fussed flossed
7. audition	audio audition audience auditorium audition
8. professional	professor profession profess professional
9. acceptance	acceptance accepted acceptance accent
10. personally	personal professional personally personally
11. expand	expanded expanding expansion expand
12. renew	remove renewal renew renewal renews
13. flurry	furry furry flurry furry flurry
14. praise	praise prize praise pride praise
15. shinnied	shinny shin shinnied shinnied shiney

TIME: _____

Check each line to see if you marked the correct word every time it appears. Make sure you can pronounce each word. Learn definitions of the words you don't know. The words by the numbers appear in the article you are going to read in this chapter.

TOTAL LINES CORRECT: _____

R: READING DRILL

A. Reading and Thinking About What You Read

Directions. Before you read most things, it's good to skim or look over what you are going to read. It helps to get your mind on the reading. In turn, it helps your comprehension. Take a minute to skim over the following article. First, read the title. Next read only the first paragraph. Last, let your eyes skim over the article just to see what you see. Don't try to read the article now. You will later. After you've skimmed over the article, come back here, and answer the questions below.

1. What do you think the article will be about? (Don't just answer, "Stevie Wonder.") _____

   _____

2. What do you think you might learn from reading this article? _____

   _____

   _____

3. What do you think the title means? _____

   _____

   _____

Now read the article. Answer each set of questions within the article. Don't worry about your spelling.

Stevie Wonder (Photograph: Wide World Photos)

STEVIE WONDER: SUNSHINE IN THE SHADOW

Linda Jacobs

[1] When Steveland Judkins Morris was born, on May 13, 1950, the doctors shook their heads and told Lula Mae Morris that her son was born blind and likely would always be that way. She broke into tears.

[2] Blind and black and poor—what kind of a life could this new infant have? In her wildest dreams, Mrs. Morris could never have imagined that her new baby would become a rich and famous musician called Stevie Wonder. At the time, all she could do was pray—and worry.

[3] Stevie himself didn't worry at all. Life was too full. He was reared among church-going people whose faith helped them bear the poverty. Music was always part of his life. He would listen to blues singer B. B. King and pound spoons or forks on any surface that faintly resembled a drum.

[4] He even ran and played with sighted children. "I didn't realize I was blind until I was about four," he says. That might sound strange. To a small child just learning about the world, it wasn't strange at all. Stevie heard and smelled and touched. As far as he knew, that was all anyone could do. That was life.

[5] He found out that he lacked something others took for granted when he came in from a backyard romp with dog manure all over his shoes and tracked it on his mother's clean floor.

[6] "Stevie," she wailed, and whacked him once in sheer frustration.

[7] "But Ma," Stevie protested, "how was I supposed to know it was there?"

[8] His mother sighed and hugged him.

[9] "You can't . . . but you shouldn't be running and jumping around like you did know."

[10] It suddenly hit Stevie that his mother would have known where to step and where not to step. Slowly, it all came together—the way his mother worried about him more than she did about the other children. The way everyone else knew what was on their plates at dinner while he had to be told. He was different.

[11] "Even then, it didn't really bother me," Stevie says. Stevie paid so little attention to his blindness that he regularly frightened his mother half out of her wits.

[12] The whack he got for tracking up the floor wasn't his last spanking. He got one the time he shinnied up a tree to steal apples. He got one the time he jumped from the roof of one shed to another, with only a

friend's voice to guide him to his target. His mother fussed and fumed and lectured, but secretly she was almost pleased with Stevie's hijinks.

[13] He was a normal kid, getting into trouble for normal pranks. Blindness wasn't holding him back. In fact, it began to look like nothing could hold him back, especially with his music.

1. Did Stevie Wonder's blindness keep him from doing things other children did? _____ How do you know? _____

_____

_____

2. Based on the last sentence you read in the article, what can you guess the next part of the story will be about? _____

_____

_____

Continue reading now.

[14] When his mother got tired of her tables being used for drums, she bought him a toy set. He played so hard that he had actually worn the toy out within a few weeks. Other toy sets followed; than an uncle added a toy harmonica, and Stevie learned to play it so quickly that everyone was amazed.

[15] Stevie taught himself to play piano as quickly as he had once learned the harmonica. With friends, he began playing rock and roll music. They held jam sessions on the front porch of Stevie's apartment building, drawing crowds of neighbors to watch and listen and clap time to the beat.

[16] "I loved that beat," Stevie says. He not only loved the beat, he was very good at making it. His talent was so big, so real, that someone just had to come along and spot it.

[17] Someone did. Ronnie White, of The Miracles singing group, was a cousin of Stevie's playmate, John Glover. Ronnie heard Stevie and promptly took him down to his recording company, Motown Records.

[18] "Give him an audition," Ronnie said. They did. All the top people at Motown got together to hear a little blind boy who wasn't even ten years old yet. At first, they were being nice. Poor kid. They didn't want to hurt his feelings.

[19] Then they heard Stevie sing and play, and nobody said "poor kid"

anymore. They were too busy congratulating themselves on finding a youngster who could be the musical talent of the decade.

[20] Stevie started going to Motown's offices every day after school. He hung around and listened to everybody else's music and grabbed every chance to play some of his own. Everyone there called him "Little Stevie."

[21] "He's a wonder boy," Clarence said one day, as he watched little Stevie dart from one instrument to another, playing each one with ease.

[22] "Wonder," somebody said. "Little Stevie Wonder."

[23] Clarence's eyes started to glow. "That's it," he said, in a voice that was filled with quiet discovery. "That's what we'll call him on his records."

[24] The name stuck and Stevie Morris became Little Stevie Wonder. He had his first hit when he was twelve years old. It was called "Fingertips" and it was a smash, topping charts all over the country.

[25] Little Stevie Wonder was on his way. He had the music he loved and more money than his family had ever seen. "It was great," Stevie says. "Half the time, I couldn't believe it was all for real."

[26] Above all, Stevie was a real professional. He recorded hit after hit —songs like "Uptight," and "My Cherie Amour." As he met more people through his work, something else began happening to him. He started taking new pride in being black.

[27] He couldn't see the color of his own skin or anybody else's. But he could hear the pain and dignity of black music, taste the difference between soul food and other dishes. He looked back on the little boy who hid his B. B. King music. That was dumb, he told himself.

[28] With that final acceptance of himself, Stevie had it all together. He knew where he wanted to go in life—now he knew who he was. More than ever, he seemed like an adult genius in a child's body.

3. What does the author mean when she says, "He started taking new pride in being black"? _____

_____

_____

4. Why did this begin to happen to him? _____

_____

_____

5. What part of Stevie Wonder's life do you think will be mentioned in

the next part of the article? _____

_____

Continue reading now.

[29] Then even the body changed. By the time he was eighteen, he topped six feet and the "Little" in front of his name sounded ridiculous.

[30] "We've got to drop it," Clarence said.

[31] "Yes," Stevie said, "I guess we do." He didn't feel little anymore. He felt grown and strong and ready to fly.

[32] And he did fly—personally as well as professionally. In 1970 he married Syreeta Wright. She was a secretary at Motown and a talented songwriter and singer in her own right. Together, Stevie and Syreeta wrote "Love Having You Around," and other tender and gentle songs.

[33] To Stevie, Syreeta was the miracle of the age. It was wonderful having someone special to share his life, his hopes. She seemed to understand his religious faith, his love of music. She respected him for his pride and for conquering his blindness.

[34] "Syreeta made me feel like expanding," Stevie says. Stevie's expansion took him in strange new musical directions. He began to resent the way Motown supervised his every move. They managed his money, his recording time, his concert schedule. Worse, they had complete control over the songs he wrote and performed. His music had to fit the Motown formula or it just wouldn't be accepted.

[35] "I want to try new things," Stevie said, but nobody listened. They patted him on the back and said that he already had a winning formula. Stick with it.

[36] But he couldn't. When his contract came up for renewal, he refused to sign unless he had artistic freedom.

[37] "You can't do this, Stevie . . . you just can't," everyone at Motown said.

[38] Stevie ached inside. These were his friends. Maybe they were right—maybe he was being disloyal. He prayed a lot and thought a lot. He remembered the time, years before, when he had been kicked out of the church choir. He had done what he felt was right then. He had to do it now.

[39] "I've got to have a new contract," he said, and the firmness in his voice left no doubt that he meant what he said.

[40] Stevie got his contract with full artistic freedom—and with more money than he'd ever dreamed of. He started making new and exciting albums like *Talking Book* and *Innervisions*.

[41] He felt good about the music, but he was nervous. What if the public didn't like his musical experiments. What if he really was wrong? To add to his worries, he and Syreeta had begun to have problems. His

Innervisions (Photograph: W. Royce Adams)

professional life and personal life were beginning to clash in a way they'd never done before.

[42] Stevie's first worry dissolved in a flurry of public acceptance and critical praise. He had been right! Everybody at Motown gladly admitted that. They even made plans to let their other artists be more involved in selecting their own music.

[43] "It was beautiful," Stevie says.

[44] But there was still the problems with Syreeta. She and Stevie still liked each other, still worked well together, but marriage was a special strain. They were seriously wondering if they could make it together when a tragedy temporarily wiped out the whole question.

[45] On August 6, 1973, Stevie was riding in a car outside of Winston-Salem, North Carolina. In a freak accident, the car hit a lumber truck. One log smashed through the windshield and jammed against Stevie's skull.

[46] After all the sirens and emergency aid and police investigation, the man who had once been Little Stevie, the Wonder boy, lay in a hospital room, deep in a coma. The coma lasted for nearly a week, while doctors fought to save his life.

[47] "We don't even know when he'll be out of danger," the doctors said. Everyone waited and prayed. Suddenly it didn't matter that Stevie was a musical genius or that he was black and proud or even that he had conquered blindness and poverty. All he had left was his faith and strong will.

[48] That turned out to be enough. He fought back from the shadow of death as he had once fought out from the shadow of blindness. He went on to give more performances, make more hit records.

[49] He still had to face the sadness of the final breakup of his marriage to Syreeta. "We just couldn't get it back together," he says.

6. Do you think it took courage for Stevie Wonder to want a new contract, or was he being foolish taking a chance with his career? _____

   Why do you think so? _____

   _____

   _____

7. Was Stevie Wonder's personal life going as well as his professional life? _____ What in the story makes you think so? _____

   _____

   _____

   _____

Continue reading now.

[50] At first, Stevie felt lost and frightened. There was an empty hole in his life. Then he met Yolanda and he found that the love he held inside him was far from spent.

[51] Today, Stevie's world is filled with Yolanda, his friends and his family. It's crowded with recording sessions and those hopelessly disorganized concerts that somehow always turn out in the end.

[52] Stevie has faith and fame, wealth and love. He understands and accepts himself—a man who has conquered his own darkness and can bring sunshine to the shadow of other lives.

8. You answered the question, "What does the title of the article mean?" before you read the article. Do you still agree with your first answer?

_____ Why? _____

_____

B. Comprehension Check

Directions. Answer the following questions without looking back at the article. Don't worry about spelling mistakes.

Recall

1. Stevie Wonder's mother cried when he was born because he was

    a. blind

    b. black

    c. poor

    d. all of the above

2. Stevie Wonder was _____ years old when he had his first hit record.

Interpretation

3. Did Stevie Wonder get special treatment as a child because he was

    blind? _____ How do you know? _____

    _____

    _____

4. Why was it courageous of Stevie Wonder not to renew his contract

    with Motown except under his own terms? _____

    _____

    _____

5. Circle the words below that fit Stevie Wonder as a person, and explain what from the article makes you think so.

    a. talented: _____

    b. famous: _____

c. strong-willed: _____

d. religious: _____

Application

6. Do you think you could overcome the problems Stevie Wonder had

and overcame, such as blindness? _____ Why? _____

_____

_____

E: EXERCISES IN VOCABULARY

A. Drills

Drill 1: Part A, The Alphabet

Directions. In the space below, print each letter of the alphabet in correct order form. You will use the alphabet list for the next drills. _____

_____

Drill 1: Part B, Expanding Words

Directions. Below are some three-letter words. Use the letters of the alphabet in front of each word to make four-letter words. The first one has been done for you.

1. and

   band, hand, land, sand, wand

2. ear

   _____

3. old

   _____

4. ake

   _____

5. ate

   _____

6. ail

   _____

Check your answers with these:
2. bear, dear, fear, gear, hear, near, pear, rear, sear, tear, wear, year.
3. bold, cold, fold, gold, hold, mold, sold, told.
4. bake, cake, fake, lake, make, rake, sake, take, wake.
5. date, fate, gate, hate, late, mate, rate.
6. bail, fail, hail, jail, mail, nail, pail, rail, sail, tail, wail.

Discuss any words you had trouble with in class. Learn from your mistakes. Don't be embarrassed by mistakes. You're here to learn.

Drill 2: Consonant Blends

Directions. Below are some letters called *consonant blends* and *consonant digraphs*. Consonant blends are two or more letters blended so that *each* letter sound is heard, such as *bl* in *black,* *pl* in *plate,* and *st* in *stamp.* Consonant digraphs are two or more letters that have one sound, such as *th* in *this* and *ch* in *chair.* Try out each consonant blend and digraph with the words below. Write in the words that can be made. Two examples are given for *ear.* You finish them.

bl cl sh sm sp sw br fl
gr qu tr sn st th ch dr

1. ear

   blear, clear

2. ake

3. ill

4. ail

Check your answers with these:
1. clear, shear, smear, spear, swear.
2. Blake, shake, spake, brake, flake, quake, snake, stake, Drake.
3. spill, swill, grill, still, chill, drill.
4. flail, grail, quail, snail, trail.

Discuss any words you had trouble with in class.

Drill 3: Vowel Sounds Review

Directions. There are four letters that are always vowels: *a, e, i, o.* There are four letters that are sometimes vowels and sometimes consonants: *u, y, w, h. U* is normally a vowel. But when it follows the letters *g* and *q*, as in *language* and *queen,* it is a consonant because of its sound. *Y* is a vowel when it sounds like it does in *bay* or *boy* and when it ends a word or syllable that does not have a vowel in it, such as *cry* or *happy.* Remember, each syllable has a vowel in it. But *y* is a consonant when it has the sound it has in *you* or *yes. W* is usually a consonant. But when it follows a vowel as in *brew, crew* or *crow,* it is a vowel. *H,* like the letter *w,* is a vowel only when it is the second letter following a vowel, as in *ah* and *oh.*

For now, let's deal with only three basic vowel sounds. Read the following examples:

SHORT VOWEL SOUND (˘)	LONG VOWEL SOUND (¯)	VOWELS WITH *r* SOUND
mat	mate	mark
pet	Pete	pert
bid	bide	bird
rot	rote	stork
cub	cube	curb

Say all the words and listen to the different vowel sounds. Then answer the questions below.

1. One vowel followed by one or more consonants (except *r*) has a ______ ______ sound.

2. One vowel followed by a consonant and a final *e* has a ______ sound.

3. One vowel followed by *r* is neither ______ nor ______ but picks up an *r* sound.

4. Check each word that has a long vowel sound:

   hide brake
   shirt flop
   child first
   bold late

5. Check each word that has a short vowel sound:

   graph chart

chorus	grab
bid	knot
winter	time

6. Check each word that has a vowel sound controlled by *r:*

chore	bird
wrong	mark
storm	spurt
flurry	ramp

Drill 4: Double Vowels Review

Directions. Read the following rules about double vowels, and then answer the questions that follow.

a. The vowels *ai, ee, oa,* and *ea,* when together in a word and followed by a consonant, usually have the long sound of the first vowel. For example:

    wait   need   road   eat

(There are some exceptions, such as *aisle* and *bear.*)

b. The vowels *ay* (*y* is sometimes a vowel), *ee, ie, ea,* or *oe* at the end of a word have the long sound of the first vowel. For example:

    bay bee tie sea toe

c. The vowels *ai, ee, oa,* or *ea* followed by the consonant *r* have an *r* controlled sound. For example:

    fair cheer roar year

In the blanks write in whether each word has a long or short vowel sound.

1. gray _____   6. hope _____

2. meat _____   7. hop _____

3. steam _____   8. bite _____

4. plan _____   9. bit _____

5. plane _____   10. steep _____

Drill 5: Words That Sound Alike

Directions. Words that sound the same but are spelled differently and have different meanings are called *homophones.* Words that have the same sound and sometimes the same spelling but differ in meaning are called *homonyms.* In the blanks, write the letter of the homonym by the numbers below.

_____ 1. weak		a. see
_____ 2. steal		b. meet
_____ 3. meat		c. deer
_____ 4. sea		d. beat
_____ 5. dear		e. week
_____ 6. beet		f. here
_____ 7. fair		g. fare
_____ 8. hear		h. hole
_____ 9. whole		i. paws
_____ 10. pause		j. steel

Check your answers: 1. e, 2. j. 3. b, 4. a, 5. c, 6. d, 7. g, 8. f, 9. h, 10. i.

B. Vocabulary Check

Part One

Directions. Circle the vowels in the words below, and in the blank following the word write in the vowel sound (long, short, silent, or with *r* sound).

1. shake _____
2. flail _____
3. spill _____
4. snail _____
5. quark _____

6. smear _____
7. quick _____
8. chorus _____
9. child _____
10. spurt _____

Part Two

Directions. Circle the consonant blends in the following words.

1. shear
2. grail
3. strong
4. flake
5. shill

6. broil
7. skill
8. drill
9. spoil
10. crank

11. chump
12. smack
13. crack
14. blame
15. shark

Part Three

Directions. In the blank, write the letter that is not heard in the following words.

1. waist _____
2. waste _____
3. tail _____
4. tale _____
5. pain _____

6. pane _____
7. sail _____
8. sale _____
9. mail _____
10. male _____

11. due _____
12. hear _____
13. here _____
14. fair _____
15. fare _____

Part Four

Directions. Explain the two rules about vowels that fit all the above words.

1. Rule about double vowels: _____

_____

_____

_____

2. Rule about final *e:* _____

_____

_____

_____

Part Five

Directions. Write a sentence correctly, using the following homonyms.

1. waist: _____

_____

2. pane: _____

_____

3. pause: _____

_____

4. steel: _____

_____

5. fare: _____

_____

NAME _____ SECTION _____ DATE _____

P: PERFECTING READING SKILLS

A. Comprehending Phrases

Directions. Define the following phrases in your own words.

1. in her wildest dreams: _____

   _____

2. helped him bear the poverty: _____

   _____

3. faintly resembled a drum: _____

   _____

4. he's a wonder: _____

   _____

5. conquered his blindness: _____

   _____

6. held his tongue: _____

   _____

7. in a firm voice: _____

   _____

8. shadow of blindness: _____

   _____

9. half out of her wits: _____

   _____

10. without a doubt: _____

_____

Discuss your answers in class.

B. Comprehending Sentences

Directions. Read each sentence, and answer the questions that follow.

1. Stevie taught himself to play the piano as quickly as he had once learned the harmonica.

   a. Does this mean Stevie learned to play the piano first? _____

   b. How do you know? _____

   _____

2. His voice was filled with quiet discovery when he said, "That's it. "That's what we'll do."

   a. Does this mean his voice was excited? _____

   b. What does "quiet discovery" mean? _____

   _____

3. "Fingertips" was a smash, topping charts all over the country.

   a. What charts are being referred to? _____

   _____

   b. Was the record successful? _____

4. Stevie felt grown and strong and ready to fly.

   a. What is meant by "ready to fly"? _____

   _____

   b. Does the sentence say he is grown and strong? _____

   _____

5. Stevie fought back from the shadow of death as he had once fought out from the shadow of blindness.

   a. What does the word *shadow* mean in the sentence? _____

   _____

   b. What can we learn about Stevie's personality from this sentence?

   _____

   _____

6. His first worry dissolved in a flurry of public acceptance and critical praise.

   a. Does this mean both the record buyers and the critics liked him?

   _____

   b. Was he worried they wouldn't like him? _____

7. Stevie seemed like an adult genius in a child's body.

   a. Is Stevie a child or an adult? _____

   b. What does the sentence mean? _____

   _____

8. Stevie Wonder is a man who conquered his darkness and can bring sunshine to the shadow of other lives.

   a. What do these words mean in the sentence:

   darkness: _____

   _____

   sunshine: _____

   _____

   shadow: _____

   _____

b. Does the sentence mean that Stevie Wonder can bring some happi-

ness to people who have problems to overcome? _____

How do you know? _____

_____

Discuss your answers in class.

C. Comprehending This Chapter

Directions. As a review of this lesson, discuss these questions in class, or write answers to them.

1. What words at the beginning of this chapter (p. 7) do you need to review with your instructor?
2. Name the vowels. What letters are always vowels?
3. What are consonant blends and consonant digraphs?
4. What do you call words that sound alike but are spelled differently and have different meanings? Name some.
5. What problems, if any, did you have with any exercises in this chapter?
6. What did you learn or relearn from the exercises in this chapter?

CHAPTER 2

Objectives

P: PREREADING DRILLS

A. Words to Know
B. Warm-up Drills

R: READING DRILL

A. Reading and Thinking About What You Read
   "Will the Real Dracula Please Stand Up?"
B. Comprehension Check

E: EXERCISES IN VOCABULARY

A. Drills
   1: Expanding Words
   2: Expanding Words
   3: Vowel Review
   4: The Schwa
   5: Homonyms, or Words That Sound Alike
B. Vocabulary Check

P: PERFECTING READING SKILLS

A. Comprehending Phrases
B. Comprehending Sentences
C. Comprehending This Chapter

OBJECTIVES

When you are finished working in this chapter, you will

1. Recognize and be able to use at least 90 percent of the vocabulary words presented in the "Words to Know" section.

2. Have developed your ability to recognize words faster.

3. Know the basic vowel sounds.

4. Know what a schwa is and its sound.

5. Know how stress marks can help you correctly pronounce words.

6. Know at least ten pairs of homonyms and be able to write sentences using them.

7. Have developed your comprehension of phrases and sentences by noting how key words and phrases are used to state the main idea.

P: PREREADING DRILLS

A. Words to Know

Directions. Here are some words that appear in the drills and article you will be reading in this chapter. Read them aloud, and learn the definitions of the ones you don't know.

1. *ancient*—old; from long ago.

   The ancient Greeks liked to tell stories.

2. *legend*—story, tale, myth.

   There are many legends about vampires, the most famous being the story of Dracula.

3. *vein*—a blood vessel that takes blood to the heart.

   Vampires like to sink their teeth into veins.

4. *convince*—to make someone believe something; persuade.

   Nancy has been convinced that there are vampires.

5. *shriek*—a loud yell or cry.

   Raul let out a shriek when the bat flew near his head.

6. *victim*—a person who has been hurt; someone tortured or put to death.

   Dracula's victim had two teeth holes in her neck.

7. *superstitious*—believing in or fearing magic or the unexplained.

   Some superstitious people believe the number thirteen brings bad luck.

8. *fiction*—something that is not true; something made up, such as a short story, play, or novel.

   The novel *Dracula*, by Bram Stoker, is a work of fiction, but some say the story is based on fact.

9. *crest*—a coat of arms, a family emblem; top of a hill.

   The crest on his shield was a dragon.

   A dragon sat on the crest of the hill.

10. *Transylvania*—a small area in Rumania in Europe.

    Dracula's home was in Transylvania.

B. Warm-up Drills

Drill 1

Directions. Some words are often misread because they are read too quickly. Read each sentence below, and look carefully at the two words under it. Then write in the correct word in the blank.

1. Howard's family _____ has two lions standing on their back legs.

   crust   crest

2. Dracula spoke with an _____ .

   ascent   accent

3. Vampires cannot see their _____ in a mirror.

   reflection   reflective

4. Don't take it seriously; the story is just _____ .

   friction   fiction

5. My Aunt Bessie has to buy a new _____ evening gown for the dance.

   formal   former

6. The victim put up a _____ before he passed out.

   straggle   struggle

7. Keep the wooden stake _____ in case we find a vampire in the coffin.

   hardy   handy

8. When she could not see her _____ in the mirror, Ruth

   imagine   image

   was convinced she was a vampire.

Check your answers and your spelling with these: 1. crest, 2. accent, 3. reflection, 4. fiction, 5. formal, 6. struggle, 7. handy, 8. image.

Drill 2

Directions. Move your eyes rapidly across each line. Mark the word by the number each time it appears on the same line. For example:

1. rear   ~~rear~~ roar ~~rear~~ roar roar
2. reared   roared ~~reared~~ roared roared ~~reared~~

Don't look back on any line. If you make a mistake, don't stop to change your answer. Keep moving on. Try to finish in less than forty seconds. Begin timing.

1. accent   ascent   ascent   accent   ascent   accent
2. stake   stake   steak   stake   steak   steak
3. coffin   coffin   coffin   coffer   coffer   coffee
4. shines   shrines   shines   shrines   shrines   shines
5. formal   formed   formed   formed   formal   formal
6. connect   correct   connect   correct   connect   correct
7. veins   vanes   vanes   veins   vanes   veins
8. image   imagine   imagine   image   image   imagine
9. struggle   straggle   struggle   struggle   straggle   struggle
10. bitten   kitten   bitter   bitten   bitter   kitten
11. tales   trails   tails   tales   tales   tails
12. their   there   their   there   their   there
13. since   since   sense   sense   since   sense
14. soul   sole   soul   sole   sole   soul
15. through   threw   through   thought   threw   through

TIME: _____

Now check each line to see if you marked the correct word everytime it appears. Make sure you know all the words and their meanings. The words by the numbers appear in the article you will read in the chapter.

TOTAL LINES CORRECT: _____

Drill 3

Directions. Follow the same directions as Drill 2. Remember, work quickly. Don't look back on a line. Don't change any mistakes you may make. It takes up time. Try to finish in less than thirty-five seconds this time.
Begin timing.

1. fiction   friction   fiction   friction   friction   fiction
2. convince   convincing   convinced   convinced   convincing   convinced
3. conqueror   conqueror   conquer   conqueror   conquer   conqueror
4. mystery   mysterious   musteriously   mystery   mastery   mystery
5. shriek   shriek   shrine   shriek   shrank   shrines
6. shines   shins   shines   shriek   shrink   shines
7. castle   coastal   coast   castle   castle   casts
8. reflection   reflective   reflection   reflects   reflective   reflection
9. creation   creative   creates   creation   creative   creatures
10. accident   accent   acidly   accident   accident   accent
11. corpse   corps   corpse   corps   corpse   corpse
12. disease   disaster   disaster   disease   disease   disaster
13. nobleman   nobleman   noble   noble   noblewoman   nobleman
14. buried   burned   buried   burned   buried   burned
15. legend   legion   legend   logger   legion   legend

TIME: _____

Check each line to see if you marked the correct word every time it appears. Make sure you can pronounce each word. Learn the meanings of all the words. The words by the numbers appear in the article you are going to read in this chapter.

TOTAL LINES CORRECT: _____

R: READING DRILL

A. Reading and Thinking About What You Read

Directions. Sometimes our minds wander when we read. It's usually because we are not ready to concentrate on what we are reading. That's why the last chapter told you to skim over what you are going to read before reading it. Do the some thing again here. First, read the title. Next, read only the first paragraph. Last, read only the first sentence of a few paragraphs until you know what the article is about. Then come back here, and answer the questions below.

1. What do you think the article will have to say about vampires? _____

   _____

   _____

2. What do you think you might learn from reading this article? _____

   _____

   _____

3. What does the title mean? _____

   _____

   _____

Now read the article. Answer each set of questions within the article. Don't worry about your spelling.

WILL THE REAL DRACULA PLEASE STAND UP?

[1] The moonlight shines into her open window. A soft breeze gently moves the curtains. Suddenly, a bat-shaped creature appears at the window. Just as suddenly, the bat turns into a tall man in a dark, formal

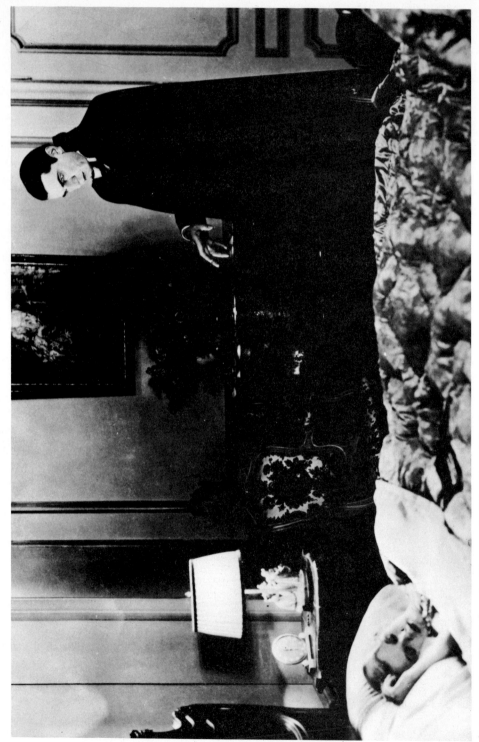

Bela Lugosi as Count Dracula (Photograph: Culver Pictures, Inc.)

evening suit with a long cape. He smiles at the beautiful woman asleep on the bed. Silently, he moves toward her. His smile gets larger, and his teeth seem to grow larger and sharper. He bends over the sleeping woman, sinks two fangs into her neck and drinks her blood.

[2] For most of us, this is Count Dracula, the vampire. He comes from Transylvania and speaks with a slight accent. He sleeps in a coffin by day and at night roams about looking for necks to bite. Dracula needs blood to stay alive, if you can call him alive. He has no soul, so he has no reflection in a mirror, yet he fears the sign of the cross. The only way to kill him is to drive a wooden stake into his heart.

[3] We get this image of vampires mainly from Bram Stoker's book *Dracula*. In 1931, the movie *Dracula* was made from Stoker's book. Bela Lugosi played Count Dracula and made famous the line, "I vant to drink your blood." Since then, many other movies and television programs have been made about Dracula or vampires like him. But there were many vampire stories long before Stoker wrote his book.

1. Based on the title and the last sentence you just read, what do you

   think the rest of the article will be about? _____

   _____

   _____

2. Why do you think bats are used in connection with vampires? _____

   _____

   _____

[4] The idea of vampires did not begin with Bram Stoker's *Dracula*. Vampire stories have been told for centuries all over the world. For example, the ancient Greeks told a story about Lamia. Lamia went mad when her children were killed. To get revenge, she started killing other children. She drank their blood and ate their flesh. Soon she turned from a beautiful woman into an ugly creature. Later on, the Greeks created a legend about a birdlike thing that flew by night, killing children and drinking their blood.

[5] Much later, in the sixteenth century, the Spanish conquerors in Mexico discovered small bats that drank blood. When the stories got back to Europe, people connected the bats with vampires. These bats were named vampire bats. Perhaps that is why modern stories connect bats, night fliers, and blood drinkers with vampires.

[6] There are many stories written about vampires that are supposedly true. A French monk named Calmet, who lived in the eighteenth

century, wrote about real vampires. He wrote about a Hungarian named Arnold Paole. Paole thought he was bitten by a vampire when he was in Turkey. He ate some dirt from the vampire's grave. Then he rubbed himself with its blood. This was supposed to be a cure.

[7] Not too long after that, Paole was killed in an accident. Within thirty days, four people died mysteriously. The people in the town remembered that Paole had been bitten by a vampire. They began to think that he might not have been cured. So they dug up his grave.

3. Do you believe Calmet's story about Paole is true? _____ Why?

_____

_____

4. What do you think they found in Paole's grave when they dug it up?

_____

_____

[8] Paole's hair and nails had grown since he was buried. His veins were filled with blood. His face was red in color. Blood was all over the cloth the body was wrapped in. This convinced the people Paole was a vampire. So they drove a stake through the body. A terrible shriek came from the corpse. Then they cut off the head and burned the body. Because they thought the four people who had died were victims of a vampire, they did the same thing to their bodies.

[9] But five years later, seventeen more people in the town died from vampires. The officials dug up the graves of everyone who had died recently. They put stakes through their hearts, cut off their heads, and burned the bodies. After that, there were no more deaths from vampires.

[10] This is only one of many vampire stories Calmet wrote about. Many of them Calmet did not believe in. He claims that many stories were started by uneducated and superstitious people. Also, in those days doctors did not know much about different diseases and causes of death. He noted that sometimes people were buried alive accidentally. Doctors weren't always sure if a person was alive or dead. Someone buried alive would struggle in the coffin. When dug up, the body would look as though it had moved around. Then people would think they had found a vampire.

5. Did Calmet believe all the vampire stories he wrote about were true?

_____

6. What made people believe Paole was a vampire? _____

_____

_____

[11] The first great fictional story about vampires was written in 1816. Byron, the famous English poet, started the story but didn't finish it. A friend of his, Dr. John Polidori, took the idea and wrote "The Vampyre." The vampire was called Lord Ruthven. The story was very popular and was later turned into a play.

[12] In the 1840s, another vampire story was written, *Varney the Vampyre, or The Feast of Blood*. The story of Varney was very popular. It is over 500,000 words long and is probably one of the longest novels ever written. But the most famous of all vampire stories is Bram Stoker's *Dracula*. Stoker's vampire is said to be based on a real character named Vlad Tepov. He was a cruel nobleman from Transylvania who lived in the fifteenth century. He hanged his enemies on sharp sticks un-

Count Dracula (played by Bela Lugosi) attacks a victim. (Photograph: Culver Pictures, Inc.)

til they died. It is reported that he killed over 100,000 people. His crest was a dragon. People often called Vlad "Dracul," which means dragon. But it can also mean "devil." Thus, in his book Stoker used the name Dracula, made him a count or nobleman like Vlad, and used Transylvania as his home. Today, tourists still visit Vlad Tepov's castle in Rumania. It is called Dracula's castle.

7. Was there a real Dracula? _____

   Explain. _____

   _____

8. When was the first fictional story about a vampire written? _____

[13] Today few people say they believe in vampires. But, as recently as 1969, an American history professor traveling in Rumania watched the burial of a young girl. He was told that she had been bitten by a vampire. The villagers were afraid the corpse would become one, too. So before they buried her, they drove a stake through her heart, just as in all the stories.

[14] For over 2,000 years there have been tales about vampirelike creatures. But then, they're only stories, right?

[15] Still, it might be best to keep a cross handy!

9. How would you feel if you saw people drive a stake through a body

   before burying it? _____

   _____

10. Do you think the author of the article is serious about keeping a

    cross handy? _____ Why? _____

    _____

    _____

    _____

B. Comprehension Check

Directions. Answer the following questions without looking back at the article. Don't worry about spelling mistakes.

Recall

1. T or F.   The first book on vampires was Bram Stoker's *Dracula.* ____

2. Who was Lamia? _____

_____

_____

3. What does the French monk Calmet have to do with vampires? _____

_____

_____

4. Who was Vlad Tepov? _____

_____

_____

Interpretation

5. In the past, doctors did not know much about diseases and how they spread. The bodies of those thought to be vampires were burned. After this, strange deaths usually stopped. Can you explain why burning those bodies was more scientific than superstitious based on what

   we know today about disease? _____

_____

_____

_____

6. How did bats become connected with vampires? _____

_____

7. Do you think some people still believe in vampires? _____ Why?

_____

_____

Application

8. Name some superstitions that you or others you know have. _____

_____

_____

_____

9. If a man who lived in the eighteenth century and believed in vampires could see people getting blood transfusions today, what would

he probably think or fear? _____

_____

_____

E: EXERCISES IN VOCABULARY

A. Drills

Drill 1: Expanding Words

Directions. Below are some three-letter groups. Make four-letter words by putting letters from the alphabet in front of each group. The first one has been done for you.

1. ath

   bath, math, path

2. unk

3. ook

4. ame

5. are

6. ore

7. ing

_____

_____

8. ead

_____

_____

_____

Check your answers with these:
2. bunk, dunk, gunk, hunk, junk, punk, sunk
3. book, cook, gook, hook, look, rook, took
4. came, dame, fame, game, lame, name, same, tame
5. bare, care, dare, fare, hare, mare, rare, ware
6. bore, core, gore, more, pore, sore, tore, wore
7. bing, ding, king, ping, ring, sing, ting, wing, zing
8. bead, dead, head, lead, read

Discuss any words you had trouble with in class. Remember, learn from mistakes.

Drill 2: Expanding Words

Directions. Below are some consonant blends you used in Chapter 1. Try adding each consonant blend to the front of the groups of letters below. Write the words that can be made on the lines. One example is given for *ank*, but there are more.

bl cl sh sm cr dr fl pl pr ch
sp st th kn qu sl sn tr wh

1. ank

   *blank,*_____

   _____

2. ack

   _____

   _____

3. ump

_____

_____

4. ame

_____

_____

_____

Check your answers with these:
1. blank, clank, shank, crank, drank, flank, plank, prank, spank, stank, thank.
2. black, clack, crack, flack, stack, knack, quack, slack, smack, track, whack.
3. clump, plump, chump, stump, thump, slump, trump.
4. blame, shame, flame.

Discuss any words you don't know or missed in class.

Drill 3: Vowel Review

Directions. Below is the vowel sound chart you learned in Chapter 1. Use it to help you answer the questions that follow.

SHORT VOWEL SOUND (˘)	LONG VOWEL SOUND (¯)	VOWELS WITH r SOUND
măt	māte	mark
pĕt	Pēte	pert
bĭd	bīde	bird
rŏt	rōte	stork
cŭb	cūbe	curb

1. Check each word that has a long vowel sound in it:

_____ shines   _____ made

_____ formal   _____ bite

_____ connect   _____ bitten

_____ sole   _____ famous

2. Check each word that has a short vowel sound in it:
_____ coffin   _____ victims

_____ struggle   _____ crest

_____ fangs   _____ legend

_____ tales   _____ accent

3. Check each word that has a vowel controlled by the *r* sound:

   _____ formal   _____ superstition

   _____ wrong   _____ shriek

   _____ storm   _____ furied

   _____ bright   _____ spurt

4. In the blanks write in whether each word has a long or short vowel sound in it.

   a. soul _____   e. veins _____

   b. struggle _____   f. shriek _____

   c. victim _____   g. steam _____

   d. castle _____   h. wait _____

Check your answers.
1. shines, sole, made, bite, famous.
2. coffin, struggle, fangs, victims, crest, legend, accent.
3. formal, storm, buried, spurt.
4. (a) long, (b) short, (c) short, (d) short, (e) long, (f) long, (g) long, (h) long.

Drill 4: The Schwa (ə)

Directions. The schwa is the symbol ə. It is used to show soft vowel sounds, usually like a soft *u* sound. In the dictionary, the schwa (ə) is the sound represented by

   a as in *a*bout
   e as in tak*e*n
   i as in Apr*i*l
   o as in lem*o*n
   u as in circ*u*s

Here are some words that have the schwa sound. Say them aloud. Notice the accent mark (') shows which syllable to stress when you say the word;

hanger (hang'ər)   ancient (ān'shənt)
legend (lej'ənd)   Transylvania (trăn'sĭl vā nē ə)

Below are two columns. In the blanks, write the letter of the word that stands for the word by the number. The first one is done for you. Some of the words in the second column are not used.

_d_ 1. let'ər   a. hanger

____ 2. mel'ən   b. later

____ 3. lāt'ər   c. color

____ 4. hang'ər   d. letter

____ 5. kol'ər   e. collar

____ 6. pə lēs'   f. melon

____ 7. hun'gər   g. please

____ 8. jen'ər ā'shən   h. hunger

                             i. police

                             j. generator

                             k. generation

Check your answers: 2. f, 3. b, 4. a, 5. e, 6. i, 7. h, 8. k.

Drill 5: Homonyms, or Words That Sound Alike

Directions. There are two columns of words below. In the blanks write the letter of the homonym by the number.

____ 1. whole   a. weight

____ 2. knot   b. wood

____ 3. rap   c. reign

_____ 4. wait   d. hole

_____ 5. piece   e. wrap

_____ 6. would   f. peace

_____ 7. rain   g. not

_____ 8. great   h. corps

_____ 9. isle   i. aisle

_____10. core   j. grate

Check your answers:
1. d, 2. g, 3. e, 4. a, 5. f, 6. b, 7. c, 8. j, 9. i, 10. h.
Learn any words you may not know.

B. Vocabulary Check

Part One

Directions. Circle the consonant blends in the words below. Some words may not have any.

1. shank
2. crank
3. bank
4. blank
5. slack

6. flame
7. fame
8. knack
9. bead
10. fare

11. flare
12. ting
13. thing
14. plank
15. quick

Part Two

Directions. In the blank following each word, write in whether the vowel sound is long, short, or controlled by the letter *r*.

1. sole _____

2. fangs _____

3. storm _____

4. shriek _____

5. bright _____

6. struggle _____

7. spurt _____

8. crest _____

9. clang _____

10. steer _____

Part Three

Directions. In the blank following the pronunciation symbols below, write what the word is. Remember, the schwa sound is a vowel that sounds like a soft *u*.

1. hung′ər _____

2. mel′ən _____

3. but′ər _____

4. dīn′ər _____

5. hol′ō _____

6. mun′ē _____

7. fūz _____

8. ān′shənt _____

9. let′ər _____

10. lĕj′ənd _____

Part Four

Directions. In the blank, write in the correct homonym from the words below the sentence.

1. Kathy ate the _____ pie!

    hole   whole

2. She didn't even save me one _____.

    peace   piece

3. It's cold; please get my _____ for me.

    wrap   rap

4. Sunday we'll walk down the _____ together.

    aisle   isle   I'll

5. Let's rent a boat and go for a _____.

    sail   sale

6. José is in the Job _____.

    corps   core

7. Don't _____ energy; turn off those extra lights.

    waist   waste

8. This is the third window _____ those boys have broken.

    pain   pane

9. The mail is _____ at eleven o'clock.

    do   dew   due

10. It's a _____ day to be alive.

    grate   great

Part Five

Directions. Write a sentence correctly, using the following words:

1. rap: _____

   _____

2. corps: _____

   _____

3. reign: _____

   _____

4. knot: _____

   _____

5. grate: _____

   _____

P: PERFECTING READING SKILLS

A. Comprehending Phrases

Directions. Define the following phrases in your own words.

1. let out a shriek: _____

   _____

2. a legend in her own time: _____

   _____

3. go to bat for him: _____

   _____

4. keep it handy: _____

   _____

5. drive a hard bargain: _____

   _____

6. blood bank: _____

   _____

7. bloodletting: _____

   _____

8. the height of success: _____

   _____

9. beat around the bush: _____

   _____

10. keep the wolf from the door: _____

_____

Discuss your answers in class.

B. Comprehending Sentences

Directions. Read each sentence, and answer the questions that follow.

1. The moonlight shines into her open window, and a soft breeze gently moves the curtains.

   a. What time of day is it? _____

   b. What is the weather probably like? _____

   _____

2. He bends over the sleeping woman and sinks two fangs into her neck and drinks her blood.

   a. What words could you use instead of "sinks two fangs"? _____

   _____

   b. Why did the woman let him do this? _____

   _____

3. In 1931, the movie *Dracula* was made from Bram Stoker's novel by the same name.

   a. Which came first, the book or the movie? _____

   _____

   b. What was the title of Stoker's book. _____

4. Calmet claims that many vampire stories were started by uneducated and superstitious people.

a. Were all vampire stories started by uneducated and superstitious

people? _____

_____

b. What key words tell you? _____

_____

5. You can kill a vampire by driving a stake through its heart, by nailing its head to its coffin, or by burning the body—the latter being the best way.

a. How many ways are there to kill a vampire? _____

b. Which is the best way? _____

6. They dug up the vampire's body and drove a stake through its heart, but the corpse only laughed and said it would use the stake as a stick to defend itself against dogs.

a. What method of killing vampires needs to be tried? _____

_____

_____

b. Does the vampire have a sense of humor? _____ How do you

know? _____

_____

7. At times moviemakers have had to strain to keep up with the people's demand for bigger and terrible monsters, but the human imagination is equal to the job.

a. Does the sentence mean that people like to be frightened in

movies? _____

b. Does the sentence mean that moviemakers will be able to answer

the demand? _____

c. Where do movie monsters come from? _____

_____

8. Though the Aztecs of Mexico had mummies, they were not as famous
   or as well known as the mummies of Egypt; but when Mexican film
   makers want to make a mummy movie, they use an Aztec mummy.

   a. Which mummies are more famous, Aztec or Egyptian? _____

   b. If you lived in Mexico, what kind of mummies would you probably

      see in mummy horror films? _____

Discuss your answers in class.

C. Comprehending This Chapter

Directions. As a review of this chapter, discuss these questions in class,
or write answers to the ones your instructor assigns.

1. What words at the beginning of this chapter (p. 37) do you need to
   review?
2. What are the basic vowel sounds?
3. What is a schwa? What sounds does it have?
4. Name at least five pairs of homonyms.
5. What comprehension problems did you have, or what do you need to
   review from the last two drills (phrase reading and sentence reading)?
6. What did you learn or relearn from the exercises in this chapter?
7. How do you feel you are doing so far with the work in this book?

CHAPTER 3

Objectives

P: PREREADING DRILLS

A. Words to Know
B. Warm-up Drills

R: READING DRILL

A. Reading and Thinking About What You Read
"My Son, the Mechanic"
B. Comprehension Check

E: EXERCISES IN VOCABULARY

A. Drills
1: Dictionary Entries
2: Dictionary Abbreviations
3: Pronunciation Keys
4: Word Meanings in Context
5: Using the Dictionary
B. Vocabulary Check

P: PERFECTING READING SKILLS

A. Comprehending Sentences
B. Comprehending Paragraphs
C. Comprehending This Chapter

OBJECTIVES

When you are finished working in this chapter, you will

1. Recognize and be able to use at least 90 percent of the vocabulary words presented in the "Words to Know" section.

2. Have developed your ability to recognize words more rapidly.

3. Understand syllabication and its usefulness in pronouncing words correctly.

4. Know and be able to understand all the information given in a dictionary entry.

5. Know and be able to use dictionary pronunciation keys.

6. Know how to find word entries in the dictionary faster than you do now.

7. Have developed your comprehension skills in recognizing main ideas, details, and figurative language in sentences and paragraphs.

P: PREREADING DRILLS

A. Words to Know

Directions. Here are some words that appear in the article in this chapter. Read the words aloud. Learn any words you don't know.

1. *pre-med student* — someone studying to get into medical school.

   After high school, she hopes the university will accept her as a pre-med student.

2. *embarrassed* — shamed, ill at ease.

   My friend was embarrassed because he didn't have money for a ticket.

3. *expose* — show, reveal, or make available or known.

   José's parents exposed him to art when he was young so that he would know something about it.

4. *alma mater* — the school or college that you have attended.

   Linda visited her alma mater when she came home.

5. *tussle* — a struggle, difficulty.

   Getting Jane up early each morning was a tussle.

6. *civil engineer* — someone who plans and builds public works, such as streets and bridges.

   There are not many women civil engineers.

7. *stewed* — worried, suffered.

   Al did something about his grades, but I just stewed about my low ones.

8. *furrier* — someone who deals in animal furs.

   Jaime asked the furrier for some scraps of fur so that he could make some fishing flies.

9. *apprentice* — a beginner; a learner or helper.

   Pat must serve two years as a carpenter's apprentice.

10. *journeyman* — someone who finished his or her apprenticeship; not a beginner, a fully trained worker.

    Pat finished her apprenticeship and is now a journeyman carpenter.

11. *bias*—preference, a leaning toward, slant, prejudice.

Because of his bias for math, my father thought I should do well in it.

12. *the humanities*—areas of study that deal with art, music, and literature.

To have a well-rounded education, you should expose yourself to the humanities.

13. *persist*—keep at it, continue, not give up.

My son never gave up; he persisted until he got the job he wanted.

14. *encounter*—(a) a meeting; or (b) to face, to come across something.

(a) When my car hit the wall, I had a close encounter with death.

(b) Terri does not want to encounter her ex-husband; so she moved.

B. Warm-up Drills

Drill 1

Directions. Some words are misread because they are read too quickly. Read each sentence below. Look carefully at the two words under it. Then write the correct word in the blank. Spell it correctly.

1. The _____ bought the three minks from him.

    funnier   furrier

2. After her mother scolded her, Carrie _____ for hours.

    strewed   stewed

3. Jerry's father is one of the biggest building _____ in town.

    contractors   contacters

4. The teacher _____ in making us do all the drills in the book.

    presented   persisted

5. That new, young apprentice has the _____ for an excellent carpenter.

    markings   makings

6. Is that the journeyman you _____ to yesterday?

referring   referred

7. The school _____ caught Jack smoking behind the PE building.

principle   principal

8. Better not lose those _____ or we won't catch any fish.

fries   flies

9. Dad wants me to expose myself to the humanities to _____ my education.

broader   broaden

10. Ben _____ he could pass without studying, but he's taking the course again this semester.

taught   thought

Check your answers and your spelling with these:
1. furrier, 2. stewed, 3. contractor, 4. persisted, 5. makings,
6. referred, 7. principal, 8. flies, 9. broaden, 10. thought.

Drill 2

Directions. Move your eyes rapidly across each line. Mark the word by the number each time it appears on the same line. For example:

1. roar   rear   rear   ~~roar~~   ~~roar~~   rear
2. struggle   straggle   ~~struggle~~   straggle   ~~struggle~~

Don't look back on any line. If you make a mistake, don't stop to change it. Keep moving. Try to finish in less than forty seconds.
Begin timing.

1. proud   pride   pride   proud   pride   proud
2. marks   marks   makes   marks   makes   makes
3. change   charge   change   charge   charge   change
4. clearly   cleanly   cleanly   clearly   cleanly   clearly
5. politics   political   politics   polite   political   politics
6. bought   brought   brought   brought   bought   bought
7. scraps   scrapes   scraps   scrapes   scrapes   scraps
8. contract   contract   contact   contact   contact   contract
9. burst   bust   burst   bust   bust   burst
10. desert   dessert   desert   dessert   desert   dessert
11. sense   sense   since   sense   sense   since
12. broaden   broader   broaden   broader   broaden   broader
13. special   special   specially   specials   specialize   special
14. exposed   exposure   expose   exposed   exposure   exposed
15. huge   hug   urge   huge   hug   urge   huge

TIME: _____

Now check each line to see if you marked the right word every time it appears. Make sure you know all the words and their meanings. All the words by the number appear in the article you will be reading in this chapter.

TOTAL LINES CORRECT: _____

Drill 3

Directions. Follow the same directions as Drill 2. Remember, work quickly. Don't look back on any line. Try to finish in thirty-five seconds or less.

Begin timing.

1. stewed	strewed stewed stewed strewed strewed
2. pre-med	premier pre-med preview pre-med premier
3. civil	civilian civil civilly civilian civil
4. admission	admire admissible admission admission
5. disappoint	disappear disappoint disappear disappoint
6. economics	economy economics economy economics
7. sense	since sense since since sense since
8. encounter	economics encounter counter economics
9. persist	persist resist persisted persistent persist
10. opinion	opening opening opinion opening opinion
11. tussle	tunnel tunnel tussle tunnel tussle
12. guarantee	guarantee guaranteed guarantee guaranteed
13. engineer	engine engineer engine engine engineer
14. embarrass	embarrass embarrassed embarrassed
15. humanity	humanly humanly humanity humanly

TIME: _____

Now check each line to see if you marked the right word every time it appears. Make sure you know all the words and their meanings. All the words by the number appear in the article in this chapter.

TOTAL LINES CORRECT: _____

R: READING DRILL

A. Reading and Thinking About What You Read

Directions. The following article is written by a father who wanted his son to go to college. But his son wanted to be a mechanic. How do you think the father feels about this? Read to find out.

MY SON, THE MECHANIC

[1] A few years ago, just before my son Luis graduated from high school, a friend asked me where Luis planned to go to college. "Don't think he is," I said. "He wants to be a mechanic."

[2] "Oh," my friend said. He seemed embarrassed and quickly changed the subject. His son had been accepted by Washington University as a pre-med student. He had often referred to his boy as "my son, the doctor." I could tell he obviously felt my son should be going to college somewhere.

[3] I understood my friend. I had always wanted my son to go to college. I did and I wanted him to go. As parents, my wife and I did all we could to prepare him for college. We read to him as a child. We took him to plays. We discussed art. As he grew older, we discussed economics and politics. But during his three years in high school, Luis was not really interested in studying or preparing for college. By the time he graduated, his grades were not high. No university would be interested in him. And he wasn't interested in any of them either.

1. Why did the friend change the subject when Luis' father said his son

    wanted to be a mechanic? _____

    _____

    _____

2. Does the father sound disappointed that Luis doesn't want to go to

    college? _____ What makes you think so? _____

    _____

A mechanic at the hood of a car (Photograph: W. Royce Adams)

[4] In fact, Luis wasn't too interested in school. He was often late for classes. Twice during his senior year, I was called into the principal's office. Luis had cut classes. All he ever got excited about that year was working on his car. I remember yelling at him once because that's all he seemed interested in doing. I told him he should get his head out from under the hood of his car. He needed to see what the world was really like.

[5] I tried to get him to study more. He has a good mind. He was always quick in math. We'd talk about going to college to become a civil engineer or maybe even an automotive engineer. I felt sure he would change his mind.

[6] But I was wrong. Luis and I just came from two different places. He thought with his hands, it seemed to me, and I thought with my head. At the time I was biased. I thought what he wanted was inferior to what I wanted for him. That made me think his way of thinking was bad.

[7] As I think back, I realize how often he showed me I was wrong. His interests just weren't mine. When he was in junior high school, I bought him a ten-speed bicycle. While I was reading the instructions, he had the bike together.

[8] Once our car broke down out in the middle of nowhere. While I stewed about what to do, Luis had the hood up and found the problem. I still don't know what was wrong or how he fixed it. But what was a tussle for me was a simple matter for Luis.

[9] He was always clever with his hands. One summer he made good money making and selling fishing flies. He went to a local furrier for scraps of rabbit or mink fur. He made contact with sporting goods stores and learned about economics his own way. With the money he earned, he bought his first car. Obviously, I persisted in urging him to save the money for college. But it was his money.

[10] Once he had a car, Luis seemed interested in nothing else. He must have taken that engine apart and put it back together a dozen times. In school, he took some automotive courses—tune-up, body shop, things like that. He didn't care about the grades but he did like the classes. I kept hoping he'd broaden his interests toward the humanities. My hopes slowly faded.

[11] Surprisingly, Luis made it through high school. His grades were average, but I knew by then he'd never be attending my alma mater.

3. What do you think of Luis so far? _____

_____

4. What do you think of the father so far? _____

_____

A mechanic repairing a car (Photograph: W. Royce Adams)

[12] Luis tried hard to find a job as a mechanic. It was difficult for a young man with no experience. But he persisted. Then, one day Luis came home excited. "I'm hired!" he shouted. "I begin as an apprentice mechanic tomorrow!" He had landed a job at a service station. He would begin helping the mechanic at the station.

[13] A change came over Luis. He became alive. Once it was a job to get him out of bed in the morning. Now he was up and out of the house by 7:30 A.M. His employers liked him. They began to give him more responsibilities. He had to handle money and deal with all types of people. He was getting an education, though not the kind I had hoped for.

[14] Luis also learned about hard bumps in life. He was laid off when business got bad. But he didn't wait for unemployment. He found another job and by the time he was 21, he was a journeyman mechanic. A year later, he and a man he worked for opened their own auto repair shop. They have more business than they can handle.

[15] I took my care in for a tune-up last week. One of Luis' customers, who didn't know who I was, told me, "That young fellow is the best mechanic in town. He does good work and he's honest."

[16] I smiled. "I know. That's my son, the mechanic."

5. Do you think Luis should have gone to college? _____ Why? _____

_____

_____

6. Is Luis' father disappointed with his son? _____ What makes

you think so? _____

_____

_____

B. Comprehension Check

Directions. Answer the following questions without looking back at the article. Don't worry about spelling mistakes.

Recall

1. T or F.   Luis did not make good grades in high school except in his auto shop classes.

2. T or F.   Luis' father went to college and wanted Luis to go, too.

3. Luis earned money to buy his first car by

    a. selling sporting goods

    b. making and selling fishing flies

    c. working as an apprentice mechanic

    d. working for his dad

4. T or F.   Luis is in business for himself.

Interpretation

5. Why does the father tell us about Luis' ability when he was young to work with his hands, such as putting the bike together and fixing his father's car? _____

   _____

   _____

   _____

6. Do you think Luis should go to college someday? _____ Why?

   _____

   _____

7. Why does Luis' father feel that Luis should have taken more of an

interest in some areas of the humanities? _____
_____
_____
_____

8. Luis' father obviously wanted Luis to go to college. How do you think
   the father feels about Luis and college now? _____
   _____
   _____

Application

9. How important is a college education to you? _____ Why? _____
   _____
   _____

10. Define education as you see it. _____
    _____
    _____
    _____

NAME _____ SECTION _____ DATE _____

E: EXERCISES IN VOCABULARY

A. Drills

Drill 1: Dictionary Entry Words

Directions. Study the dictionary entry below. Notice what you can learn from a dictionary entry.

Spelling and number of syllables | How to pronounce the word | What part of speech | Different definitions

plat·ter (plăt′ər) *n.* **1.** A large, shallow dish or plate, used especially for serving food. **2.** A meal or course served on such a dish. **3.** *Slang.* A phonograph record. [Middle English *plater,* from Norman French, from Old French *plate,* PLATE.]

Entry word — Special meanings — History or origin of the word

Copyright © 1973 by Houghton Mifflin Company. Reprinted by permission from *The American Heritage Dictionary of the English Language.*

Now answer the following questions. Don't worry about the questions you can't answer. More exercises will cover these things and so will your instructor. This drill will let you know what you need to learn about dictionary entries.

1. What is meant by a dictionary entry word? _____

_____

2. How many syllables does the entry word have? _____

3. Does the first syllable have a long or short vowel sound? _____

4. Can you guess what part of speech the entry word is? _____

5. How many definitions are given for the entry word? _____

6. From what language did the entry word originally come? _____

7. Write a sentence using each of the definitions correctly:

Definition 1: _____

_____

Definition 2: _____

_____

Definition 3: _____

_____

Check your answers with these:
1. An entry word is the word to be defined. 2. two, 3. short, 4. noun (the next drill has more on this), 5. three, 6. Old French, 7. Answers will vary. Have your instructor check them.

Drill 2: Dictionary Abbreviations

Directions. All dictionaries use marks and symbols to save space. These keys are explained in the front of dictionaries. Here are a few examples. Study them. Then answer the questions below.

PARTS OF SPEECH

adj.	adjective
adv.	adverb
conj.	conjunction
inf.	infinitive verb
n.	noun
pron.	pronoun
pl.	plural
v.	verb

WORD ORIGIN

Am.	American
A.S.	Anglo-Saxon
Brit.	British
D.	Dutch
Fr.	French
G.	German
Gr.	Greek
L.	Latin
M.E.	Middle English
O.E.	Old English

What do these symbols or abbreviations mean?

1. L. _____   4. adv. _____

2. v. _____   5. Am. _____

3. G. _____   6. O.E. _____

7. conj. _____

8. Gr. _____

9. n. _____

10. pl. _____

Check your answers with these:
1. Latin, 2. verb, 3. German, 4. adverb, 5. American, 6. Old English,
7. conjunction, 8. Greek, 9. noun, 10. plural.

Drill 3: Pronunciation Keys

Directions. All dictionaries have a Pronunciation Key. It is explained in the front of the dictionary. Good dictionaries have sample keys at the bottom of each page or every other page. Study the key below. Then answer the questions that follow.

PRONUNCIATION KEY

ā	as in *rate, mail*	ū	as in *fuse, cute*
ă	as in *rat, band*	ŭ	as in *cut, bump*
ē	as in *be, keep*	oo̅	as in *moon, tool*
ĕ	as in *bet, dress*	ŏŏ	as in *book, look*
ī	as in *bite, pie*	ə	as in *beautiful* (bū'tə fəl)
ĭ	as in *bit, ill*	′	accent mark to show which
ō	as in *go, stole*		syllable is stressed
ŏ	as in *rot, plot*		

Part A. Place the correct mark over the vowels in the following words. Draw a line through a vowel not sounded.

1. cute   3. coal   5. gold   7. streak

2. clock   4. grain   6. pray   8. bleed

Part B. When we pronounce a word with two or more syllables, we accent one syllable. The word *platter* has two syllables (plat'ter). We accent the first syllable when we say the word. Say the word *platter*, and notice where it is stressed. Below are some words divided into syllables. Place the accent mark on the syllable that is the accented syllable. The first one has been done for you.

1. hap'pen   4. sev en   7. des ert

2. let ter   5. in deed   8. mark ings

3. dol lar   6. con tact   9. ex posed

10. bi as
11. prin ci pal
12. en coun ter
13. ap pren tice
14. con trac tor
15. hu man i ties

Part C. Sound out the pronunciation symbols in the column on the left. Match each set of symbols with the word it represents from the column on the right. The first one has been done for you.

f 1. ĕm băr′əs   a. economics

_____ 2. chānj   b. engineer

_____ 3. ĕn′jə nĭr′   c. political

_____ 4. prĭn′sə pəl   d. expose

_____ 5. fŭr′ē ər   e. stewed

_____ 6. ĕk ə nŏm′ĭks   f. embarrass

_____ 7. kŏn′trăk tər   g. civil

_____ 8. pə lĭt′ĭ kəl   h. journeyman

_____ 9. ĕk spōz′   i. change

_____10. ăd mĭsh′ən   j. opinion

_____11. pŏl′ə tĭks   k. politics

_____12. jŭr nē mən   l. admission

_____13. ə pĭn′yən   m. furrier

_____14. stood   n. contractor

_____15. sĭv′əl   o. principal

Check your answers with these:
Part A. 1. cūte̸, 2. clŏck, 3. cōạl, 4. grăĭn, 5. gōld, 6. prāy, 7. strēạk, 8. bleed.
Part B. 2. let′ter, 3. dol′lar, 4. sev′en, 5. in deed′, 6. con′tact, 7. des′ert, 8. mark′ings, 9. ex posed′, 10. bi′as, 11. prin′ci pal, 12. en count′er, 13. ap pren′tice, 14. con′trac tor, 15. hu man′i ties.
Part C. 2. i, 3. b, 4. o, 5. m, 6. a, 7. n, 8. c, 9. d, 10. 1, 11. k, 12. h, 13. j, 14. e, 15. g.

Drill 4. Word Meanings in Context

Directions. Below is the dictionary entry for *plate*. Notice how many definitions it has. Read each sentence below the dictionary entry. In the blanks, write the number of the definition that best fits the way *plate* is used in the sentence.

plate (plāt) *n.* **1.** A smooth, flat, relatively thin, rigid body of uniform thickness. **2. a.** A sheet of hammered, rolled, or cast metal. **b.** A very thin plated coat or layer of metal. **3. a.** A flat piece of metal forming part of a machine: *a boiler plate.* **b.** A flat piece of metal on which something is engraved. **4. a.** A thin piece of metal used for armor. **b.** Armor made of this. **5.** *Abbr.* **pl.** *Printing.* **a.** A sheet of metal, plastic, rubber, paperboard, or other material converted into a printing surface, such as an electrotype or stereotype. **b.** A print of a woodcut, lithograph, or other engraved material, especially when reproduced in a book. **c.** A full-page book illustration, often in color and printed on paper different from that used on the text pages. **6.** *Abbr.* **pl.** *Photography.* A light-sensitive sheet of glass or metal upon which an image can be recorded. **7.** *Dentistry.* A thin metallic or plastic support fitted to the gums to anchor artificial teeth. **8.** *Architecture.* In wood-frame construction, a horizontal member, capping the exterior wall studs, upon which the roof rafters rest. **9.** *Baseball.* Home base, usually a flat piece of heavy rubber. Also called "home plate." **10. a.** A shallow dish in which food is served or from which it is eaten. **b.** The contents of such a dish. **c.** A whole course served on such a dish. **11.** Food and service for one person at a meal: *dinner at a set price per plate.* **12.** Household articles covered with a precious metal, such as gold or silver. **13.** A dish passed among a congregation for the collection of offerings. **14.** *Sports.* **a.** A dish, cup, or other article of silver or gold offered as a prize. **b.** A contest, especially a horse race, offering such a prize. **15.** A thin cut of beef from the brisket. **16.** *Anatomy & Zoology.* **a.** A thin, flat layer or scale. **b.** A platelike part or organ. **17.** *Electronics.* **a.** Any electrode, as in a storage battery or capacitor. **b.** The anode in an electron tube. —*tr.v.* **plated, plating, plates.** **1.** To coat or cover with a thin layer of metal. **2.** To armor. **3.** *Printing.* To make a stereotype or electrotype from. **4.** To give a glossy finish to (paper) by pressing between metal sheets or rollers. [Middle English, from Old French, from feminine of *plat,* flat, from Vulgar Latin *plattus* (unattested), from Greek *platus,* broad, flat. See **plat-** in Appendix.*]

Copyright © 1973 by Houghton Mifflin Company. Reprinted by permission from *The American Heritage Dictionary of the English Language.*

_____ 1. Turk ordered the hot plate for lunch.

_____ 2. Grandpa went to the dentist to get his plate fixed.

_____ 3. The boiler plate was too hot to touch.

_____ 4. The pitcher threw the ball right over home plate.

_____ 5. I was embarrassed at church when they passed the collection plate because I had no money.

_____ 6. The battery plate was cracked.

_____ 7. The book was supposed to have a colored picture on this page, but the printer lost the plate.

_____ 8. It was a cheap cup; the gold plate is already coming off.

_____ 9. Three plates were broken during the earthquake.

_____ 10. The armor plates on the plane made it fly more slowly.

Check your answers with these.
1. 10c, 2. 7, 3. 3a, 4. 9, 5. 13, 6. 17a, 7. 5c, 8. 2b, 9. 10a, 10. 4a.

Drill 5: Using the Dictionary

Directions. For this drill you will need a dictionary. Look up each word below, and find the information asked for.

1. _run_

   a. Number of syllables _____

   b. Pronunciation marks _____

   c. Parts of speech _____

   d. List at least four different meanings that you understand.

      1. _____

      2. _____

      3. _____

      4. _____

2. _company_

   a. Number of syllables _____

   b. Pronunciation marks _____

   c. Parts of speech _____

d. List at least four different meanings that you understand.

1. _____

2. _____

3. _____

4. _____

3. *spirit*

   a. Number of syllables _____

   b. Pronunciation marks _____

   c. Parts of speech _____

   d. List at least four different meanings that you understand.

   1. _____

   2. _____

   3. _____

   4. _____

4. *principal*

   a. Number of syllables _____

   b. Pronunciation marks _____

   c. Parts of speech _____

   d. List at least four different meanings that you understand.

   1. _____

   2. _____

   3. _____

   4. _____

5. *principle*

    a. Number of syllables _____

    b. Pronunciation marks _____

    c. Parts of speech _____

    d. List at least four different meanings that you understand.

        1. _____

        2. _____

        3. _____

        4. _____

6. *personality*

    a. Number of syllables _____

    b. Pronunciation marks _____

    c. Parts of speech _____

    d. List at least four different meanings that you understand.

        1. _____

        2. _____

        3. _____

        4. _____

Discuss your answers in class. Make sure you understand all definitions.

B. Vocabulary Check

Part A

Directions. In the space below, write at least five things a dictionary entry tells you about a word.

1. _____

2. _____

3. _____

4. _____

5. _____

Part B

Directions. Place a stress mark on the syllable in the words below that is most strongly accented or stressed. The first one has been done for you.

1. en gi neer'
2. en coun ter
3. con trac tor
4. ex posed
5. in deed

6. civ il
7. jour ney man
8. hu man i ty
9. bi as
10. o pin ion

Part C

Directions. Write a sentence correctly, using each of the words below.

1. spirit: _____

_____

2. encounter: _____

_____

3. bias: _____

_____

4. opinion: _____

_____

5. plate: _____

_____

6. exposed: _____

_____

7. alma mater: _____

_____

8. stewed: _____

_____

9. apprentice: _____

_____

10. tussle: _____

_____

P: PERFECTING READING SKILLS

A. Comprehending Sentences

Directions. Read the sentences below. In the blanks, write what you think the underlined phrase means. If you don't know, guess. Don't spend too much time on any one sentence.

1. His daughter Nan is *the apple of his eye.*

   _____

2. The doctor said Mel will be *back on his feet* in a week or so.

   _____

3. You can't *back out* on me now! You promised you'd go.

   _____

4. May's not *a bad egg;* let's invite her to come along.

   _____

5. I tried *to catch his eye* at the concert, but he didn't see me.

   _____

6. If Carter wins, it will be a *feather in his cap.*

   _____

7. *Eat your heart out,* Hank; I'm taking Juana to the dance.

   _____

8. *Keep your chin up;* maybe she'll go with you the next time.

   _____

9. I told Dad that if he'd *foot the bill,* I'd go to college.

   _____

10. John never seems to know when I'm *pulling his leg*.

_____

11. Judy really has *a lot on the ball*.

_____

12. I borrowed money from a loan shark, and now I'm *paying through the nose*.

_____

13. What Peg said really *rubbed me the wrong way*.

_____

14. When I see Peg, I'm going to give her a *piece of my mind*.

_____

15. If John doesn't get a job soon, we won't be able *to keep the wolf from the door*.

_____

Discuss your answers in class.

B. Comprehending Paragraphs

Directions. Read the following paragraphs, and answer the questions that follow them.

1. In the past fifteen years, every state in the union has passed a law against child-beating. Now, many states are also passing laws against wife-beating. Wife-beating is a bigger problem than most people think. A bill has been sent to Congress that would set up centers to help the beaten wife.

    a. What is the paragraph's main idea?

    _____

    _____

b. Does the paragraph tell what states have laws against wife-

beating? _____

_____

2. Helping wives who have been beaten by their husbands is not easy. Beaten wives don't like to give information or discuss their problems with their doctors or the police. But a recent issue of the *Journal of the American Medical Association* has a report that shows battered wives are afraid to tell the truth about how they are hurt by their husbands.

a. Is it easy to help a woman who has been beaten by her husband? __

_____

b. Why? _____

_____

c. Why do you think beaten wives don't often tell their doctors or the

police? _____

_____

3. Doctors say these are the early signs of alcoholism. One, is what they call "pattern drinking." That means the person has, for example, a drink every night when he/she gets home. Or, maybe the person drinks only on weekends. The time of drinking has a pattern to it. Two, the drinker can't stop the habit even when he/she tries. Third, the drinker changes from one drink to another. Fourth, the drinker argues with family and friends. Fifth, the drinker loses interest in things that don't involve drinking.

a. What is the main idea of the paragraph?

_____

b. If a person fits several of the five points listed, what does that

mean? _____

_____

4. The page boys who work for the House of Representatives are angry. They say that the page girls who work with them get to quit work at 6 P.M., even when the House has night sessions. But the page boys have to work until the House quits no matter how late. It is explained that the page girls leave early because Washington, D.C., is not a safe city at night. It is feared the girls will get mugged. But the page boys refuse to accept this since three page boys have already been mugged in the city.

a. What is the main idea of the paragraph? _____

_____

_____

b. Where is this taking place? _____

c. What do you think the page boys want? _____

_____

_____

d. Why do you agree or disagree with the page boys? _____

_____

_____

5. The need for secretaries has not dropped. Secretaries know that jobs are easy to find just about everywhere. Because of this, they are being more aggressive on their jobs. Secretaries are no longer letting their bosses just send them for coffee, empty ashtrays, or other such jobs. Ellen Cassedy, head of a Boston group called "9 to 5" says, "We hope to embarrass businessmen into not doing this kind of stuff any more and to encourage women to refuse."

a. What is this paragraph about? _____

_____

b. Why are secretaries being more aggressive on the job? _____

_____

_____

c. What does the name of the group "9 to 5" mean? _____

_____

_____

d. Can you guess what the "9 to 5" group does or wants to do for its

members? _____

_____

_____

Discuss your answers in class.

C. Comprehending This Chapter

Directions. As a review of this chapter, discuss these questions in class. Your instructor may want you to write answers to some or all questions.

1. What words at the beginning of this chapter (p. 65) do you need to review?
2. Explain what a dictionary entry is.
3. What information, besides a word's meaning, does a dictionary entry have?
4. What is meant by contextual meanings of words?
5. Why is it important to know how to use a pronunciation key?
6. What comprehension problems, if any, did you have in the last two drills?
7. What did you learn or relearn from this chapter?

UNIT 1
CHECK TEST (Chapters 1–3)

Part 1: Word Knowledge

A. Directions. Mark the vowels in the following words as long (ā), short (ĕ) or controlled by *r* ((ir)).

1. hide
2. grab
3. time
4. chore
5. first

6. ramp
7. spurt
8. storm
9. chorus
10. flop

11. tail
12. smear
13. child
14. mail
15. male

B. Directions. In the blanks below, write the letter of the word that stands for the symbols by the number.

_____1. pə lēs

_____ 2. mel'ən

_____ 3. lāt'ər

_____ 4. hang'ər

_____ 5. kol'ər

a. letter

b. later

c. melon

d. mellow

e. please

f. police

g. hanger

h. hunger

i. collar

j. color

C. Directions. Below are some words. In the blanks, write each word in syllables. Then place the accent mark on the syllable that gets stressed. For example: contractor: *con' trac tor*

1. principal: _____

2. encounter: _____

3. bias: _____

4. apprentice: _____

5. humanities: _____

Part 2: Word Usage

Directions. Write a sentence using correctly the following words:

1. waste: _____

_____

2. pause: _____

_____

3. fare: _____

_____

4. wail: _____

_____

5. decade: _____

_____

6. core: _____

_____

7. frustration: _____

_____

8. audition: _____

_____

9. flurry: _____

_____

10. romp: _____

_____

11. superstitious: _____

_____

12. ancient: _____

_____

13. bias: _____

_____

14. journeyman: _____

_____

15. persist: _____

_____

Part 3: Reading Comprehension

Directions. Read the following short selections on studying, and answer the questions that follow each selection. Try not to look back for an answer unless you have to. You will have only twenty minutes to read and answer all questions.

A. Almost every job requires the use of tools and skills. Carpenters, mechanics, plumbers, painters, to name just a few, develop their skill with tools. Doctors, artists, teachers, sports people, all have certain tools and skills they must learn to use well. Students are no different. They, too, have tools and skills they must develop to do well in school. These are known as "study skills." Study skills include managing study time, listening, note-taking ability, good reading comprehension, and knowledge on how to take tests. Though many students try to do well in college, they do not have the proper skills. They don't know how to study, and they don't take time to develop study skills.

1. What is the main idea of the paragraph? _____

   _____

   _____

2. What study skills do students need to develop? _____

   _____

   _____

3. Why do some students not do well in school even though they try? ___

   _____

   _____

4. Would the author probably be for or against study skills classes being

   taught at colleges? _____ Why? _____

   _____

B. Managing study time is a big problem with many students. Here are some hints that may help. First, try to study a subject at the same time and place each day. If, for example, you study English at the same hour and place each day, you soon will be in the habit of thinking about English at that time. You will get in the mood to study English more quickly that way. Do this with each of your subjects. Second, don't spend more than an hour in one sitting on a subject. Studies show that more is learned in four one-hour sessions over a four-day period than one long six-hour study session. The mind can only soak up so much at one time. Third, take rest periods often. Don't sit and cram a lot in at once. A five-minute break whenever you feel tired or restless is best. Then study until you need another break. Fourth, don't study when you are tired. In fact, studies prove that the best learning technique is to review what you have already learned a few minutes before a class begins. Then study the new material learned in class as soon afterward as possible.

5. What is the main idea of the paragraph? _____

_____

_____

6. Why should you study a subject at the same time and place each day

if possible? _____

_____

7. Why should you not study one subject for more than an hour at a time

with breaks? _____

_____

_____

8. What is the method suggested as the best learning technique? _____

_____

_____

UNIT 2

CHAPTER 4

Objectives

P: PREREADING DRILLS

A. Words to Know
B. Warm-up Drills

R: READING DRILL

A. Reading and Thinking About What You Read
   "Jobs and Personalities"
B. Comprehension Check

E: EXERCISES IN VOCABULARY

A. Drills
   1: Root Words
   2: Prefixes
   3: Suffixes
   4: Syllables and Vowels
   5: Context Clues and Dictionary Definitions
B. Vocabulary Check

P: PERFECTING READING SKILLS

A. Comprehending Sentences
B. Comprehending Paragraphs
C. Comprehending This Chapter

OBJECTIVES

When you have finished with this chapter, you will

1. Recognize and be able to use at least 90 percent of the vocabulary words listed in the "Words to Know" section.

2. Know what root words are and how to identify them.

3. Know how to use the prefixes *dis, im, in, ir,* and *un.*

4. Know how to use the suffixes *able, ly, ic, ful, ness,* and *less.*

5. Have reviewed syllabication and know what makes a syllable.

6. Be able to define the term *context clues.*

7. Know how to use context clues to help you select the proper dictionary definition of a word that has more than one meaning.

8. Have developed your reading comprehension skills in the areas of identifying main ideas, inferences, and sequence of events.

P: PREREADING DRILLS

A. Words to Know

Here are some words that are in the article you will be reading in this chapter. Read them aloud and learn the definitions of the ones you don't know.

1. *personalities* —the qualities or traits that make us individuals.

   The world is full of many different personalities.

2. *vocational* —having to do with jobs, employment, career.

   Pablo teaches wood shop at a vocational school downtown.

3. *artistic* —having talent in painting, acting, singing, designing, and so on.

   Jane's artistic talents won her a scholarship to an art school.

4. *conventional* —common, usual, regular, ordinary, everyday.

   It is conventional to tip waitresses and waiters.

5. *enterprising* —energetic, clever, resourceful.

   Sam's an enterprising businessman.

6. *intellectual* —(a) learned, intelligent (adj.); (b) scholar, "brain" (n.).

   (a) This magazine is not a very intellectual one. (b) Very few intellectuals ever run for president.

7. *realistic* —true, genuine, accurate, possible.

   His ideas for getting rich are not very realistic.

8. *social* —(a) friendly, polite, human (adj.); (b) a gathering of people (n.).

   (a) I live in a very social neighborhood. (b) Are you going to the church social?

9. *sensitive* —sore, nervous, touchy, aware of others' feelings.

   Shirley is very sensitive about her grades.

10. *conservative* —careful, cautious, conventional.
    After his fall, Tom was more conservative on his skateboard.

11. *practical* —workable, able to do, attainable.

    The practical way to get the sink fixed is to hire a plumber.

12. *shrewd*—clever, intelligent, tricky.

Because my uncle is a shrewd businessman, people want his advice.

13. *confident*—sure, certain.

The coach feels confident our team will win.

14. *impatient*—irritable, not tolerant, lacking control.

Manuel gets impatient with people who litter.

B. Warm-up Drills

Drill 1

Directions. Some words are often misread because they are read too quickly. Read each sentence below, and look carefully at the two words under it. Then write in the correct word in the blank.

1. Our _____ are what make us different.

     personality   personalities

2. Sam attended a _____ school for two years.

          vocational   vacation

3. Maria's _____ talents won her first prize in the art show.

       artistry   artistic

4. The teacher's solution was _____ and not as original as we had hoped.
                              conventional   conversational

5. Jerry's sister is so _____ she cries if you look at her cross-eyed.
             sensitivity   sensitive

6. My father is very _____ with his money; I have to come up with a really sad tale to get any from him.
            conservation   conservative

7. Mrs. Cobb is _____ she will get a raise this month.

         confined   confident

8. That used-car salesman was more _____ than I was and took advantage of me.

shrewd   shrew

9. If you are _____, you won't take more classes than you can handle.

practice   practical

10. Be _____; you can't get away with robbing that bank!

realist   realistic

Check your answers and your spelling with these:
1. personalities, 2. vocational, 3. artistic, 4. conventional, 5. sensitive,
6. conservative, 7. confident, 8. shrewd, 9. practical, 10. realistic.

Drill 2

Directions. Move your eyes rapidly across each line, and mark the word by the number each time it appears on the same line. For example:

1. laugh   tough   laugh   tough   laugh   tough
2. right   night   night   right   right   night

Don't look back on any line. If you make a mistake, don't stop to change your answer. Try to finish in less than thirty seconds.
Begin timing.

1. social   sociable   social   sociable   sociable   social
2. artistic   artistic   artist   artist   artistic   artist
3. vocational   vacation   vacation   vocational   vacation
4. shrewd   shrew   shrew   shrewd   shrew   shrewd
5. realistic   realize   realistic   realist   realistic   realize
6. impatient   impatient   important   important   impatient
7. sensitive   sensible   sensitive   sensitive   sensible   senses
8. conservative   conservation   conservation   conservative
9. practical   practice   practically   practice   practical
10. create   creative   create   creative   create   creative
11. choices   chances   choices   chances   chances   choices
12. impression   impression   impatient   impression   impatient
13. describe   describe   description   describe   description
14. eager   easy   eager   eager   easy   eager
15. personality   personalities   personalities   personality

TIME: _____

Now check each line to see if you marked the correct word every time it appears. Make sure you can pronounce the words and know their definitions. The words by the numbers all appear in the article you are going to read in this lesson.

TOTAL LINES CORRECT: _____

Drill 3

Directions. Follow the same directions as in Drill 2. Remember, work quickly, don't look back on a line, and don't change any mistakes you may make. Try to finish in less than thirty seconds.
Begin timing.

1. confident	confide confident confidential confide
2. image	imagine imagine image imagine imagine
3. curious	curious curiosity curiosity curious
4. scenes	screens screens scenes screens screams
5. ordinary	ordinarily ordinary ordinarily ordinary
6. enterprising	enterprise enterprise enterprising
7. through	thought through through thought thought
8. impression	impression impressed impression impress
9. accountant	accountable accountant accountable
10. status	statue status statue statue status
11. critical	critical critics critical critics critics
12. characteristic	character characteristic character
13. politics	politician politics polite politics polite
14. independent	independence independent dependent
15. involved	involvement involve involved involve

TIME: _____

Check each line to see if you marked the correct word every time it appears. Make sure you can pronounce the words and know their definitions. The words by the numbers appear in the article you are going to read in this lesson.

TOTAL LINES CORRECT: _____

R: READING DRILL

A. Reading and Thinking About What You Read

Directions. Take a minute to skim over the following article. First, read the title; next, read only the first paragraph; and last, read each of the six headings. That's all. Don't read anything else. Then come back here, and answer the questions below.

1. What do you think this article will be about? _____

   _____

2. What do you think you might learn from reading this article? _____

   _____

   _____

Now read the article, and answer each set of questions within the article.

JOBS AND PERSONALITIES

[1] In his book *Making Vocational Choices*, John Holland says there are six basic types of personalities. First, he groups people by their likenesses and differences. Then he describes what most people are like in each of the six groups. Holland does this because he feels we can make better job choices if we know our own personality type. His six personality types are "Artistic," "Conventional," "Enterprising," "Intellectual," "Realistic," and "Social."

1. From what you have read so far, did you guess correctly what the

   point of the article is about? _____

2. Why does Holland describe personality types in a book about making

   vocational choices? _____

   _____

3. What do you think the rest of the article will be about? _____

_____

Group One: The Artistic Type

[2] Very creative people of the Artistic type are good in art, crafts, music, and writing. They are not too sociable and like to daydream and create things. Politics and sports don't interest them much. They would rather be admired for their creative talents. People of the Artistic type think of themselves as independent, not ordinary, thoughtful, sensitive, and self-confident. They admire painters, writers, actors, and creative people.

[3] Maria is an example of an Artistic type. She's quiet and calm, but gets much from life. Her artistic eye sees things others don't see in common events and scenes. Maria is admired for her ability to see beauty. Her taste in things is not common or ordinary. She could do well as an artist or a writer. In fact, she is paying her way through college by selling her paintings and leather craft work.

A bulldozer dumping its load into a truck (Photograph: W. Royce Adams)

4. What words that describe the Artistic type also describe you? _____

_____

5. What jobs do you think the Artistic type person would enjoy? _____

_____

Group Two: The Conventional Type

[4] Those in the Conventional group usually give good first impressions. They are conservative, neat, a little stubborn, somewhat sociable, and interested in money matters. They are not too interested in religious matters or sports. They do well in business, economics, and math.

[5] The Conventional type think of themselves as hardworking, practical, careful, and shrewd. They like to solve problems. Though they don't think they are good leaders, they do think they are dependable and stick to what they start. They usually become involved in business, usually as office managers, bookkeepers, or accountants.

[6] Jake is an example of the Conventional type. People like him when they first meet him. He's a good B student and considered a solid guy. He doesn't talk much but gets the job done. Jake likes to read the financial page, especially the stock market report. He is more concerned with national politics than most students. After graduating, Jake wants to become a bookkeeper, get married, and provide the best for his family.

6. What words that describe the Conventional type also describe you? __

_____

7. Why do you think the Conventional types do well in business? _____

_____

Group Three: The Enterprising Type

[7] Adventurous, energetic, and eager describe the Enterprising type. People in this group like to lead. They are interested in all kinds of things—more than the other five groups. They think of themselves as good leaders and speakers, happy, confident, and "go-getters." Their interests are in power, status, and politics. The Enterprising types want to be their own boss and like to take risks. They are good as salespersons, business promoters, and politicians.

[8] An example of the type is Mike. Mike couldn't wait to get out of school and into business. After working as a used car salesman for two years, he borrowed money and started his own used car lot. This did not

Sharks being unloaded from a boat (Photograph: W. Royce Adams)

work out for Mike, but he was quick to switch to selling insurance. He now has his own agency and is doing well. However, he is thinking of getting into the real estate game, too.

8. What words that describe the Enterprising type also describe you? ____

_____

9. Can you think of other jobs in which the Conventional type might do

well? _____

_____

Group Four: The Intellectual Type

[9] Intellectual types are not too interested in physical things. They prefer dealing with words and ideas. Their self-image includes being thoughtful, curious, self-controlled, critical, independent, bright, and

not very social. Intellectuals want to do well in school and usually like reading, music, art, science, and foreign languages.

[10] People in this group don't like physical force. They feel that power comes through knowledge. Intellectual types are not usually good in sports or physical skills. They stay away from crowds and are not usually good leaders because they put themselves down socially.

[11] Tom is an example of the Intellectual type. He's a good student who likes to do extra reading. He writes good essays and enjoys the research and writing of term papers. Tom can be talking away about a subject he likes, not even aware that others aren't interested. His goal is to get a Ph.D. in science. Though he is not too concerned with people around him, he is concerned about society's progressing.

10. What words that describe the Intellectual type also describe you? ___

_____

11. Why would people in this group probably not be interested in auto

mechanics? _____

_____

Group Five: The Realistic Type

[12] The Realistic types are conservative in their actions and dress. They think of themselves as "solid citizens." They are usually practical and dependable, but not too talkative or interested in being leaders. People in this group are not "social animals." They tend to prefer physical activities: working with tools, machines, crafts or being involved in sports or the outdoors.

[13] An example of a Realistic type person is Sally, a PE major. Sally is physically strong and likes to jog and play tennis and volleyball. She goes backpacking every chance she gets. Sally would much rather go to a football or baseketball game than to a movie. She only reads what she needs to in order to get by, but she finds a challenge in problems that have practical answers. She talks straight and can be trusted. Sally is always ready to help a person in need.

12. Do you have any of Sally's characteristics? _____

_____

13. What type jobs would Sally like to have? _____

_____

Group Six: The Social Type

[14] Obviously, the Social types like people. They are often less interested in sports or mechanics and prefer student politics, church and community service, speech and dramatics. Social types are usually popular and do well in school.

[15] This group's self-image includes being dependable, practical, energetic, cheerful, and helpful. They admire such people as lawyers, judges, and politicians. Usually, the social type become social workers, teachers, politicians, or missionaries.

[16] Sara is the Social type. She's involved in student government, holds a class office, and works part time in a hospital. Because she is so busy, she usually gets *C*'s even though she could do better if she spent more time studying. Sara feels she does a good job as a class officer and at the hospital. She gets impatient with people who don't take seriously what she does.

14. What words that describe the Social type also describe you? _____

A Hawaiian fisherman fixing a lobster pot (Photograph: W. Royce Adams)

15. Do you think Sara would make a good dental assistant? _____

Why? _____

_____

[17] These descriptions of the six types of personalities can help give you an idea of your own personality. But most people don't fit only into one group. Your own personality may fit more than one type. No one group is any better than another. What is important is that you learn more about yourself so you can make the right vocational choice and prepare for it. That's the point of John Holland's book, *Making Vocational Choices*.

15. Of the six types of personalities, which one or ones do you think you

fit? _____ Why? _____

B. Comprehension Check

Directions: Answer the following questions without looking back at the article. Don't worry about spelling mistakes.

Recall

1. Name as many of the personality types that you can remember.

   a. _____   d. _____

   b. _____   e. _____

   c. _____   f. _____

2. If you wanted to learn more about the six personality types, what

   could you read that would give more information? _____

   _____

Interpretation

3. What is the point of the article? _____

   _____

   _____

4. T or F.   Most people fit into one of the six personality types.

Application

5. What did you learn from the article about your personality and the

   jobs you might enjoy most? _____

   _____

   _____

   _____

E: EXERCISES IN VOCABULARY

A. Drills
Drill 1: Root Words

Directions. Many words are made by adding endings, prefixes, and suffixies to root words. A root word is a word from which others are formed. For example:

create $\boxed{s}$ creat $\boxed{ion}$ $\boxed{un}$ creat $\boxed{ive}$

(an ending)   (a suffix)   (a prefix and suffix)

The root word is *create*. Sometimes, as in the case of *create*, the final letter of a root word is dropped when a suffix is added. In the blank following each of the three word groups below, write the root word. Sometimes, you may need to add a letter to the root because it was dropped when the suffix was added, as in *creation (create)*.

1. artist, artistic, unartistic _____

2. conventions, conventional, unconventional _____

3. unreal, realist, realistic _____

4. dependable, dependent, independent _____

5. personality, impersonal, personalities _____

6. impractical, practically, practicalness _____

7. unenjoyable, enjoyable, enjoys _____

8. ordinarily, extraordinary, ordinariness _____

9. accountant, accountable, accounts _____

10. conservation, conservative, conserving _____

Check your answers: 1. art, 2. convention, 3. real, 4. depend, 5. personal, 6. practical, 7. enjoy, 8. ordinary, 9. account, 10. conserve.

Drill 2: Prefixes

Directions: Prefixes, like *un, in,* and *dis,* are word parts that are added to the beginning of a word to make a new word. For example, the prefix *un* placed in front of *creative* makes the word *uncreative.* The following prefixes generally mean "not" or "opposite of."

     dis im in ir un

See how many of the following words can be changed to new words by adding one of the prefixes above. Write the correct prefix in the blank.

1. _____practical

2. _____patience

3. _____sensitive

4. _____social

5. _____replaceable

6. _____regular

7. _____personal

8. _____artistic

9. _____approve

10. _____dependable

Check your answers: 1. im, 2. im, 3. in, 4. un, 5. ir, 6. ir, 7. im, 8. un, 9. dis, 10. un.

Drill 3: Suffixes

Directions. Suffixes, like *y, ness,* and *ic,* can be added to the end of a word to make a new word. For example, the suffix *ness* added to the end of the word *shrewd* makes the word *shrewdness.* Add the correct suffixes from the list below to the following words. There may be more than one answer for some.

     able ly ic ful ness less

1. sensitive _____

2. sociable _____

3. depend _____

4. practical _____

5. impatient _____

6. doubt _____

7. point _____

8. personal _____

9. realist _____

10. creative _____

Drill 4: Syllables and Vowels

Directions. Every word has at least one vowel in it. The vowels, remember, are *a, e, i, o, u,* and sometimes *y, w,* and *h.* Every syllable in a word also has at least one vowel in it. For example:

Art is a one syllable word with the vowel *a.*

Artist has two syllables (ar'-tist); the vowel *a* is in the first syllable; the vowel *i,* in the second syllable.

Artistically has five syllables (ar-tis'-ti-cal-ly); the vowel *a* is in the first syllable; *i,* in the second; *i,* in the third; *a,* in the fourth; and *y,* in the fifth because the *y* sounds like the vowel *e.*

In the blanks following each word below, divide the words into syllables, and underline the vowels in each syllable. The first one is done for you.

1. conventional

   con - ven - tion - al

2. independent

3. uncommonly

4. impersonal

5. conservation

6. impractical

7. accountant

8. personality

_____

9. curiousness

_____

10. realistic

_____

Check your answers: 2. in-de-pen-dent, 3. un-com-mon-ly, 4. im-per-son-al, 5. con-ser-va-tion, 6. im-prac-ti-cal, 7. ac-count-ant, 8. per-son-al-i-ty, 9. cur-i-ous-ness, 10. re-al-is-tic.

Drill 5: Context Clues and Dictionary Definitions

Directions: Below are some dictionary entries. Notice that more than one definition is given for each word entry. For instance, _conservative_ has six definitions.

Read each sentence on the next page. Write in the blanks the number of the dictionary definition that best fits the way the underlined word is used in the sentence.

con·ser·va·tive (kən-sûr′və-tiv) _adj._ 1. Tending to favor the preservation of the existing order and to regard proposals for change with distrust. 2. _Capital_ C. Adhering to or characteristic of the Conservative Party of the United Kingdom. 3. _Capital_ C. Adhering to or characteristic of Conservative Judaism. 4. Moderate; prudent; cautious: _a conservative estimate._ 5. Traditional in manner or style; not showy: _a conservative suit._ 6. Tending to conserve; conserving; preservative. —_n._ 1. A conservative person. 2. _Capital_ C _Abbr._ **C.** A member or supporter of the Conservative Party of the United Kingdom. 3. _Capital_ C. _Abbr._ **C.** A member or supporter of the Progressive-Conservative Party of Canada. 4. A preservative.

con·ven·tion·al (kən-vĕn′shən-əl) _adj._ 1. Developed, established, or approved by general usage; customary. 2. Conforming to established practice or accepted standards. 3. Marked by or dependent upon conventions, to the point of artificiality. 4. _Art._ Represented in simplified or abstract form. 5. _Law._ Based upon consent or agreement; contractual. 6. Of or having to do with an assembly. 7. Using means other than nuclear weapons or energy. —**con·ven′tion·al·ism'** _n._ —**con·ven′tion·al·ist** _n._ —**con·ven′tion·al·i·za′tion** _n._ —**con·ven′tion·al·ly** _adv._

im·pres·sion (im-prĕsh′ən) _n._ 1. The act or process of impressing. 2. The effect, mark, or imprint made on a surface by pressure. 3. An effect, image, or feeling retained as a consequence of experience. 4. A vague notion, remembrance, or belief. 5. _Printing._ **a.** All the copies of a publication printed at one time from the same set of type. **b.** A single copy of this printing. 6. _Dentistry._ An imprint of the teeth and surrounding tissue in material such as wax or plaster, used as a mold in making dentures or inlays. —See Synonyms at **opinion.**

sen·si·tive (sĕn′sə-tiv) _adj._ 1. Capable of perceiving with a sense or senses. 2. Responsive to external conditions or stimulation. 3. Susceptible to the attitudes, feelings, or circumstances of others. 4. Quick to take offense; touchy. 5. Easily irritated: _sensitive skin._ 6. Readily altered by the action of some agent: _sensitive to light._ 7. Registering very slight differences or changes of condition. Said of an instrument. 8. Fluctuating or tending to fluctuate, as stock prices. 9. Dealing with classified governmental information, usually involving national security: _a sensitive post in the State Department._

so·cial (sō′shəl) _adj._ 1. **a.** Living together in communities. **b.** Characterizing such communal living. **c.** Of or pertaining to society. 2. Living in an organized group or similar close aggregate: _social insects._ 3. Involving allies or members of a confederacy. 4. Of or pertaining to the upper classes. 5. Sociable; fond of the company of others. 6. Intended for convivial activities. 7. Pertaining to or occupied with welfare work: _a social worker._ —_n._ An informal social gathering, as of the members of a church congregation. Also called "sociable."

_____ 1. The army was told to use only *conventional* weapons.

_____ 2. For a superstar, her dress seems rather *conventional*.

_____ 3. My sister Ellen mixes with a higher *social* class than I do.

_____ 4. Cows are very *social* animals.

_____ 5. Harry's hearing is very *sensitive*, and he can hear sounds I can't.

_____ 6. Harry is also very *sensitive* about his big ears.

_____ 7. Because he is so *conservative*, I bet he does not approve of the tax reform bill.

_____ 8. Susan's new dress is very *conservative*.

_____ 9. The dentist took a wax *impression* of my teeth.

_____ 10. After the meeting, I got the *impression* Helen was angry.

Check your answers: 1. 7, 2. 2, 3. 4, 4. 2, 5. 2, 6. 4, 7. 1, 8. 5, 9. 6, 10. 3.

B. Vocabulary Check

Part One

Directions. Write a sentence using each of the words below. You may change endings to fit the context of your sentence.

1. vocational: _____

_____

2. artistic: _____

_____

3. conventional: _____

_____

4. independent: _____

_____

5. impersonal: _____

_____

6. conservative: _____

_____

7. sensitive: _____

_____

8. impressions: _____

_____

9. realistic: _____

_____

10. enterprising: _____

_____

Part Two

A. *Directions.* Cross out any prefixes or suffixes on the words below, and define the root word only. Sometimes the final letter of the root word has been dropped when a suffix is added.

1. uncreative_____

2. unrealistic_____

3. unsociable _____

4. impatient _____

5. shrewdly _____

B. *Directions.* Use the correct prefix to change the following words to mean the opposite of what they mean.

   dis im in ir un

1. ____sensitive   6. ____conventional

2. ____artistic   7. ____accountable

3. ____common   8. ____personal

4. ____dependable   9. ____appoint

5. ____perfect   10. ____replaceable

P: PERFECTING READING SKILLS

A. Comprehending Sentences

Directions. Read each sentence, and answer the questions that follow it.

1. The train was delayed ten hours because of heavy snows on the tracks.

   a. Does the sentence mean the train will be late? _____

   b. What one word tells you this? _____

2. If you are practical, Mario, don't plan to enroll in more classes than you can handle with your present 25-hour work week.

   a. Does the sentence mean that Mario is enrolled in school now? _____

   b. Is Mario working now? _____

3. It is never a good idea to repeat rumors because they may not be true.

   a. Does this mean you should repeat true rumors? _____

   b. Does this mean you should not repeat gossip? _____

4. After his fall, Carlos was more cautious on his skateboard.

   a. Did Carlos probably get hurt when he fell? _____

   b. Why? _____

5. Very few intellectuals are ever elected president of the United States.

   a. Does this mean few intellectuals ever become president? _____

   b. Does this mean few intellectuals ever run for the office of president? _____

   c. Could this mean voters don't want an intellectual for a president?

   _____

6. Shortly after the Zuñi Indians finished their rain dance, thunder was heard and lightning flashed.

    a. Who did the dancing? _____

    b. What type of dance was it? _____

    c. When was the thunder heard? _____

    d. Did it rain right after the dance? _____

7. The Skytrain DC-10 lifted high into the sky and began its polar flight to London.

    a. What is a Skytrain DC-10? _____

    b. Where is it going? _____

    c. What route is it taking? _____

    d. How long has the flight been so far? _____

    _____

8. Maria was so sensitive about the burn hole in her skirt that she kept her hand over it so no one could see it.

    a. Was Maria embarrassed? _____

    b. What was burned? _____

    c. How was it burned? _____

    _____

    d. Does Maria smoke? _____

Discuss your answers in class.

B. Comprehending Paragraphs

Directions: Read each paragraph, and answer the questions that follow it.

1. Whereas I thought with my head, Jack seemed to think with his

hands. I believed his way of thinking was inferior. I was wrong. For instance, on camping trips, he saved me from disaster many times. Jack would have no trouble building fires or a shelter. My wife said that if she were stranded on a desert island, she'd rather have Jack along than me.

a. Whom is the paragraph about? _____

b. What is the paragraph about? _____

_____

c. Of the six personality types, what type is Jack? _____

_____

d. Does the "I" think he is better than Jack? _____

2. Most food would be usable after a nuclear attack. Radiation passes through food and does not hurt it. The danger would be swallowing fallout particles that were on the food itself or on the can or package. These can be wiped or washed off.

a. Would it be all right to eat canned food after a nuclear explosion?

_____

b. Why? _____

c. What is the real danger with radiation and food? _____

_____

3. Most people speak at about 125 words per minute. Yet we think about four or five times faster. It's like a speaker's being in the slow lane and the listener's being in a fast lane on a highway. Often we want to leave the speaker behind. That's why we need to learn listening concentration.

a. How fast do we speak? _____

b. How fast do we think? _____

c. Why does this sometimes cause listening problems? _____

_____

4. *The Dictionary of Occupational Title* (or *DOT*) is a two-volume book that describes and classifies all the different jobs in America today. *DOT* is a good aid to students, counselors, employers, and others. It lists all job fields, the tasks they involve, and the skills needed for the job. Looking through *DOT* can help people be aware of jobs available and what skills or training they should get in order to qualify for a particular job.

    a. What does *DOT* stand for? _____

    b. What kind of book is *DOT?* _____

    _____

    c. Why is it helpful? _____

    d. To whom is it helpful? _____

    _____

5. Mrs. Gomez was tired. It seemed like weeks since she had slept. Her twelve-year-old daughter, Alicia, was resting quietly now. Mrs. Gomez knew from experience that she would sleep well for hours. She got up from her chair by the bed. She checked Alicia's breathing once more, then went to bed for some rest.

    a. Why was Mrs. Gomez tired? _____

    b. What time of day is it? _____

    c. Is this the first time Alicia has been so ill? _____

    d. What's wrong with Alicia? _____

C. Comprehending This Chapter

Directions: As a review of this chapter, discuss these questions in class. Your instructor may want you to write answers to some.

1. What words at the beginning of this chapter (p. 103) do you need to review?
2. Discuss which of the six types of personalities you think you fit. Share your reasons in class.
3. What are root words? Give an example.
4. What are prefixes? Give an example.

5. What are suffixes? Give an example.
6. What are the vowels?
7. What is meant by "words in context"?
8. Discuss any comprehension problems you had in the last two drills.

CHAPTER 5

Objectives

P: PREREADING DRILLS

A. Words to Know
B. Warm-up Drills

R: READING DRILL

A. Reading and Thinking About What You Read
   "The Great Babe" by Leo Durocher
B. Comprehension Check

E: EXERCISES IN VOCABULARY

A. Drills
   1: Homonyms
   2: Prefixes
   3: Suffixes
   4: Compound Words
   5: Words in Context
B. Vocabulary Check

P: PERFECTING READING SKILLS

A. Comprehending Sentences Using Idioms
B. Comprehending Paragraphs
C. Comprehending This Chapter

OBJECTIVES

When you have finished with this chapter, you will

1. Recognize and be able to use at least 90 percent of the vocabulary words listed in the "Words to Know" section.

2. Be able to name and use at least six pairs of homonyms used in this chapter.

3. Know the various meanings of the prefix *in* and name at least six words using it.

4. Know the meanings and how to use the suffixes *ish, er, or, ful, able,* and *ible.*

5. Know at least five compound words.

6. Know how to define the term *compound words.*

7. Know how to use context clues in sentences to define key words.

8. Have developed your reading comprehension skills by applying *who, what, why, when, where,* and *how.*

9. Have developed your reading comprehension skills in drawing inferences and understanding idiomatic expressions.

P: PREREADING DRILLS

A. Words to Know

Directions. Here are some words that appear in the article in this chapter. Read them aloud. Learn the definitions of the ones you don't know.

1. *aspects*—sides, parts, points.

   Please think about all aspects of the job before you take it.

2. *dominate*—rule, control, govern.

   Babe Ruth dominated the game of baseball.

3. *resent*—to have bad feelings toward someone or something.

   Nobody seemed to resent the Babe for dominating the game.

4. *accomplishments*—things done, completed, finished; achievements.

   Lynn received an award from the office staff for her many accomplishments.

5. *pitter-patter*—fast tapping sounds.

   The constant pitter-patter upstairs kept me awake all night.

6. *pigeon-toed*—having the toes of the feet point inward, like a pigeon's.

   His pigeon-toed walk was hard to copy.

7. *trot*—to move faster than a walk; to jog; to hurry.

   After the Babe hit the ball out of the park, he trotted around the bases.

8. *swagger*—to walk as if you are important; to walk as though you are proud of yourself.

   No one minded his swagger because they knew he was kidding.

9. *infield flies*—short high balls that batters hit near the bases rather than far out in the outfield.

   People didn't come to see the Babe hit infield flies; they wanted home runs.

10. *lunge*—to move forward suddenly.

    The catcher lunged for the foul ball.

11. *exaggerate*—to make bigger than it is; to go beyond the truth.

She is exaggerating what actually happened.

12. *invariably*—goes on and on; constantly.

Leo invariably tries to improve his game.

13. *instinctive*—coming from within; unlearned ability; happening without thinking.

The Babe's ability to steal bases was instinctive.

14. *charisma*—a quality, manner, or power that attracts. People such as Burt Reynolds, Barbra Streisand, and Muhammad Ali have charisma.

B. Warm-up Drills

Drill 1

Directions. Read each sentence below. Under each sentence are two words. Write the correct word in the blank.

1. Don't _____; you weren't hurt that badly.

                swagger   exaggerate

2. Larry made a _____ for the little girl and grabbed her before she fell.
                lunge   trot

3. Lucy's ability to serve at tennis seems _____.

                               instinctively   instinctive

4. The class is tired of all _____ of the course.

                  aspects   resentments

5. The feeling of _____ toward the teacher is growing.
                accomplishments   resentment

6. Don't try to _____ the dance floor.

                resent   dominate

7. Let's break into a _____ and get there sooner.

swagger   trot

8. For some reason, Joe's answers are _____ wrong.

instinctively   invariably

9. Her manager is using her _____ personality to maker her a superstar.

charisma   charismatic

10. John took his prize, bowed to the audience, and _____ off the stage.

dominated   swaggered

Check your answers with these:
1. exaggerate, 2. lunge, 3. instinctive, 4. aspects, 5. resentment,
6. dominate, 7. trot, 8. invariably, 9. charismatic, 10. swaggered.

Drill 2

Directions. Move your eyes rapidly across each line. Mark the word by the number each time it appears on the same line. Don't look back on any line. If you make a mistake, don't stop to change your answer. Try to finish in less than thirty seconds.
Begin timing.

1. resent	recent resent recent resent recent
2. pockets	pockets pocket pocket pockets pocket
3. concern	concert concert concern concert concern
4. thought	ought thought ought ought thought
5. great	grate great grate great grate
6. pitter	patter pitter patter patter pitter
7. trot	troop troop trot trot troop
8. waist	waste waste waste waist waist
9. stagger	swagger stagger swagger stagger swagger
10. applaud	applause applied applaud applause applied
11. charged	charged charged changed changed change
12. since	sense sense since since sense
13. thrill	trill thrilling thrill trill thrillingly
14. super	super supper super supper supper
15. field	filed filed filed field field

TIME: _____

Check each line to see if you marked the correct word every time it appears. Make sure you can pronounce *all* the words and know their meanings. The words by the numbers appear in the article in this chapter.

TOTAL LINES CORRECT: _____

Drill 3

Directions. Follow the same directions as in the last drill. Move quickly. Don't look back on a line. Don't stop to change mistakes. Try to finish in thirty seconds or less.
Begin timing.

1.	dominate	dominate dominated dominate dominoes
2.	champ	champ chump champion champ chump
3.	trying	frying trying frying frying trying
4.	aspects	aspire aspects aspire aspire aspects
5.	twirl	twins twit twirl twins twirl
6.	belt	felt belt belt felt felt felt
7.	shuffle	shuffle swagger swagger shuffle shudder
8.	stole	stool stool stole stole stool
9.	seem	seam seam seam seem seem
10.	watch	watch whack watch whack whoosh
11.	worth	worry worry worth worry worth
12.	holler	holy holler hole holly holler
13.	bench	bunch bunch bench bench bunch
14.	break	brake brake break brake break
15.	ankles	angles ankles angles ankles angels

TIME: _____

Check each line to see if you marked the correct word every time it appears. Make sure you know all the words. The words by the numbers appear in the article in this chapter.

TOTAL LINES CORRECT: _____

R: READING DRILL

A. Reading and Thinking About What You Read

Directions. The article you are going to read is about Babe Ruth. "The Babe," as he was called, is one of the all-time baseball greats. Until Hank Aaron beat his record, Babe Ruth was the home-run champ. The author of the article is Leo Durocher. He is a famous baseball personality, remembered mostly as the manager of the New York Giants in the early 1950s. He knew many great baseball stars. Here he writes about Babe Ruth.

Look at the title of the article. What type of things will the author

need to say, based on the title? _____

_____

Now read the article, and answer the questions as they appear.

"THE GREAT BABE"
Leo Durocher

[1] Babe Ruth dominated that team totally. He dominated it on the field, and he dominated it even more off the field. He made more money by far than anybody else, and nobody resented it, because we knew he was putting money in all of our pockets. There has never been anything like Babe Ruth, because everything about him was bigger than life.

1. Does the author resent Babe Ruth because he dominated the team

and the field? _____ How do you know? _____

_____

2. What does the phrase "he was putting money in all our pockets"

Babe Ruth (Photograph: Wide World Photos)

mean? _____

_____

[2] As far as I am concerned, there is only one all-time home-run champ and that's Babe Ruth. All right, Henry Aaron went to bat 2,890 more times in order to hit one more home run. All you have to do is use your common sense. I'm not trying to take anything away from Henry Aaron. Long before anybody even thought he had a shot at the record I had been saying that they ought to put Henry Aaron in the Hall of Fame right now. While he was still playing. Henry Aaron is a great all-around ballplayer who, among his other accomplishments, hit a lot of home runs. If you appreciate baseball in all its finer aspects, he has been a pleasure to watch.

3. Why does the author make the point about Henry Aaron's going to

   bat more times than Ruth? _____

_____

4. What does the author think of Henry Aaron as a ballplayer? _____

_____

[3] Babe Ruth was ***The Sultan of Swat***
[4] Babe Ruth was ***THE BAMBINO***
[5] Babe Ruth was what you came to see!!!!
[6] It was like going to a carnival, with Babe as both the star per-former and the side-show attraction. Hell, that's what we called him: "You big ape." He was what a home-run hitter was supposed to look like. Wide, flat nose. Big feet. Little ankles. Belly hanging over his belt. All he had to do was walk on to the field and everybody would applaud. The air became charged with electricity. You just felt that something great was going to happen.
[7] He'd twirl that big 48-ounce bat around in little circles up at the plate as if he were cranking it up for the Biggest Home Run Ever Hit— *you felt that* — and when he'd hit one he would hit it like nobody has hit it before or since. A mile high and a mile out. I can see him now, as I did so many times, just look up, drop the bat and start to trot, the little pitter-patter pigeon-toed, high-bellied trot that seemed to say, I've done it before and I'll do it again, but this one was for you. (Henry Aaron has a good home-run trot too; it's probably the most colorful thing about him. He holds his elbows up high, if you've ever noticed, and kind of swaggers from the waist up while he's kind of shuffling from the waist down.)

5. Why does the author say that going to a baseball game with Babe Ruth playing was like going to a carnival? _____

_____

_____

6. Why are paragraphs 3, 4, and 5 so short?

_____

_____

_____

[8] The Babe didn't even have to hit a home run to thrill you. He would hit infield flies that were worth the price of admission. The fielder would holler, "I got it," and he'd wait . . . and wait . . . and then he'd begin to stagger and finally he'd make a wild lunge. The ball would land fifteen feet away from him, and the Babe would be standing on second base with a big grin on his face.

[9] You'll think I'm exaggerating when I say that it was a thrill to see him strike out. But not if you ever saw him. He would take that big swing of his and you could hear the whole stands go *Whooooossshhhh!* And then break out into wild applause as he was walking back to the bench.

[10] Charisma counts. Charisma is what takes a superstar and turns him into a super-superstar. I've never seen a charismatic ballplayer who didn't make the team better than it figured to be, for the same reason that a charismatic actor makes any play he is in better than it should be. There is just something about these people that carries everybody else along with them.

[11] There's no question about it, Babe Ruth was the greatest instinctive baseball player who ever lived. He was a great hitter, and he had been a great pitcher. The only thing he couldn't really do was run, but when he went from first to third—or stole a base for you—he invariably made it because he instinctively did the right thing.

7. The last two paragraphs are written around two words that the author uses to explain why Ruth was so great. What are they? _____

_____

8. How does the author's use of description help readers understand why old-timers think Babe Ruth was so great? _____

_____

_____

B. Comprehension Check

Directions. Answer the following questions without looking back at the article.

Recall

1. T or F.   The author has respect for Henry Aaron as a great baseball player.

2. T or F.   Babe Ruth hit infield flies that excited people as much as his hitting home runs, according to the author.

3. T or F.   The author claims it was a thrill to watch Babe Ruth strike out.

4. Which of the following terms are used by the author to describe Ruth?
   a. the Sultan of Swat
   b. the Bambino
   c. "You big ape"
   d. side-show attraction

Interpretation

5. Why does the author compare Ruth with Henry Aaron? _____

_____

_____

6. Why do you think Babe Ruth had charisma? _____

_____

_____

7. Do you think the author thinks Babe Ruth is a better ballplayer than

Henry Aaron? _____ Why? _____

_____

Application

8. Name people living today that you feel have charisma. _____

_____

_____

9. In your mind are there any "super-superstars" like Babe Ruth living

today? _____ If so, who? _____

_____

E: EXERCISES IN VOCABULARY

A. Drills

Drill 1: Homonyms

Directions. Read each sentence below. In the blank, write the correct homonym from under the sentence. Use the dictionary if necessary.

1. I needed to borrow _____ dictionary.

    there   their   they're

2. The police were on the _____ of the accident five minutes after the call.

    seen   scene

3. Please don't take the _____ on my desk.

    stationary   stationery

4. Thelma doesn't know _____ or not her horse will get well.

    weather   whether

5. She needs a new _____ for her horse.

    bridal   bridle

6. As the song says, "Nobody knows the trouble I've _____."

    scene   seen

7. _____ one should he buy?

    Witch   Which

8. The dog was on the _____ of the escaped convict.

    cent   scent

9. Because Terry was a _____, the man in the liquor store

minor   miner

would not sell him any booze.

10. Mr. Diaz did not have enough _____ to start his own business.

capital   capitol

11. I confess my story was not _____ correct.

holy   wholly

12. The cat tore the _____ on my skirt.

seem   seam

13. The convict was caught and sent back to his _____.

sell   cell

14. It's not nice to _____ at someone.

stair   stare

15. Look in that _____ brown box in the corner.

plane   plain

Check your answers with these:
1. their, 2. scene, 3. stationery, 4. whether, 5. bridle, 6. seen,
7. which, 8. scent, 9. minor, 10. capital, 11. wholly, 12. seam, 13. cell,
14. stare, 15. plain.

Drill 2: Prefixes

Directions. In the last chapter you learned the prefixes *dis, im, in, ir,* and *un.* They all mean "not" or "opposite of." The prefix *in* can also mean "in" or "into," as in *indoors.* In the blank in front of the words below, write whether the prefix *in* means "not" or "in." The first one has been done.

1. _**not**_ inactive
2. _____ infield
3. _____ independent
4. _____ ingrown
5. _____ informal
6. _____ indirect
7. _____ insane
8. _____ inhale
9. _____ insecure
10. _____ inside

11. _____ inexact
12. _____ inland
13. _____ inexpensive
14. _____ inhuman
15. _____ indent
16. _____ inexact
17. _____ incapable
18. _____ inspect
19. _____ invisible
20. _____ invade

Check your answers with these:
2. in, 3. not, 4. in, 5. not, 6. not, 7. not, 8. in, 9. not, 10. in,
11. not, 12. in, 13. not, 14. not, 15. in, 16. not, 17. not, 18. in,
19. not, 20. in.

Drill 3: Suffixes

Directions. Study the suffixes below and their meanings. Then answer the questions that follow.

SUFFIX	DEFINITION	EXAMPLES
able, ible	can be done	enjoyable, payable
ance, ence	state of being	acceptance, dependence
tion, ion	state of being	protection, collection
ful	full of	skillful, peaceful
er, or	degree; person	greater, inspector
ish	like; belong to	childish, Spanish

A. Make the following words mean "people" by adding the correct suffix from above.

1. sail _____

2. farm _____

3. conduct _____

4. swim _____

5. employ _____   8. teach _____

6. act _____   9. visit _____

7. wait _____   10. govern _____

B. Make the following words mean "full of" by adding the correct suffix from above.

1. peace _____   6. success _____

2. pain _____   7. hand _____

3. doubt _____   8. distrust _____

4. bash _____   9. purpose _____

5. skill _____   10. mind _____

C. Change the following words to mean "like" or "belong to" by adding the correct suffix.

1. self _____   6. Jew _____

2. fool _____   7. shrew _____

3. Scot _____   8. fever _____

4. style _____   9. wolf _____

5. green _____   10. sheep _____

D. Change the following words by adding the correct suffix. (Don't use *ed* or *ing*.)

1. accept _____   6. differ _____

2. assist _____   7. protect _____

3. deliver _____   8. perish _____

4. convert _____   9. reverse _____

5. depend _____   10. response _____

Check your answers with these. Notice the need to change the spellings of some words.

A. 1. sailor, 2. farmer, 3. conductor, 4. swimmer, 5. employer, 6. actor, 7. waiter, 8. teacher, 9. visitor, 10. governor.

B. 1. peaceful, 2. painful, 3. doubtful, 4. bashful, 5. skillful, 6. successful, 7. handful, 8. distrustful, 9. purposeful, 10. mindful.

C. 1. selfish, 2. foolish, 3. Scottish, 4. stylish, 5. greenish, 6. Jewish, 7. shrewish, 8. feverish, 9. wolfish, 10. sheepish.

D. 1. acceptance, 2. assistance, 3. deliverance, 4. convertible, 5. dependable, 6. difference, 7. protection, 8. perishable, 9. reversible, 10. responsible.

Drill 4: Compound Words

Directions. Compound words are words that are made up of two or more words. Below are some compound words. Fill in the blanks in the sentences with the correct compound word.

sailboat	overcook
mailman	nightgown
password	seaman
bathroom	tablecloth
newspaper	handbag

1. Tibb is in the room where you take a bath (_____).

2. Do you want to buy a powerboat or a boat that sails (_____

   _____)?

3. You'll need to be a good man of the sea (_____) in

   order to sail that one.

4. Mom bought a new covering for the table (_____)

   when she went shopping.

5. While shopping, she almost had the bag she carries her money in

   (_____) stolen.

6. Mom also bought me a new gown to sleep in (_____)

   because mine was ruined in the washer.

7. I was left to finish dinner, but I am afraid I will let the meat cook too long (_____).

8. The sentry wanted the soldier to give the word that allows him to pass through the gate (_____), but the soldier forgot it.

9. The man who brings the mail (_____) is late today.

10. The daily paper that contains news (_____) is going up to fifteen cents a copy.

Check your answers with these:
1. bathroom, 2. sailboat, 3. seaman, 4. tablecloth, 5. handbag,
6. nightgown, 7. overcook, 8. password, 9. mailman, 10. newspaper.

Drill 5: Words in Context

Directions. Below are some words with more than one definition. In the blanks, write in which definition fits the way the sentence uses the word.

1. *meet:* to gather together; to pay; to be introduced to; to come face to face.

   a. The club will meet every Tuesday. _____

   _____

   b. The teacher wanted to meet my parents. _____

   _____

   c. The company is afraid he won't meet his debts. _____

   _____

2. *cross:* angry; mix or mingle; a symbol; to go from one side to another.

   a. The little girl was afraid to cross the street. _____

   _____

   b. In lab, we crossed a cat with a fish and got a catfish! _____

   _____

   c. What's Al so cross about? _____

3. *heavy:* weighty; intense; severe; sad; boring.

   a. Late last night we got a heavy rain. _____

   _____

   b. The heavy snow on the limb of the tree caused it to break. _____

   _____

   c. The movie was so heavy to bear that I wanted to leave. _____

   _____

4. *form:* instruct or develop; type; shape; take shape; paper or document.

   a. The clouds began to form over the mountains. _____

   _____

   b. Parents have much to do with forming a child's attitude about life.

   _____

   c. Please sign this form on the broken line. _____

   _____

5. *spirit:* mood or feelings; ghost; energy.

   a. We need to show the team our school spirit. _____

   _____

b. My spirits have been high ever since Jan said she'd go out with me.

_____

c. Some say an evil spirit still lives in that old house. _____

_____

Check your answers with these:
1. a. gather together,   b. to be introduced to,   c. pay.
2. a. to go from one side to the other,   b. mix,   c. angry.
3. a. severe,   b. weighty,   c. boring, *but could be* sad *or* intense.
4. a. shape,   b. instruct *or* develop,   c. paper *or* document.
5. a. energy,   b. mood *or* feelings,   c. ghost.

B. Vocabulary Check

Part A

Directions. Write a sentence for each of the following words.

1. scene: _____

   _____

2. stationery: _____

   _____

3. bridal: _____

   _____

4. capital: _____

   _____

5. scent: _____

   _____

Part B

Directions. In the blanks, write the prefix *in* if it can change the root words below.

1. ____ formal   6. ____ dent

2. ____ payable   7. ____ secure

3. ____ dependence   8. ____ resent

4. ____ lunge   9. ____ field

5. ____ variable   10. ____ capable

Part C

Directions. Circle the suffixes in the following words. Draw a line under any compound words.

1. selfish
2. painful
3. homemade
4. wolfish
5. tenderness
6. distrustful
7. manpower
8. preference
9. securely
10. tapdance
11. careless
12. waiter
13. conductor
14. deliverance
15. handful

Part D

Directions. Answer the following questions.

1. What prefix can mean "in" or "not"? _____

2. What suffixes are used to make words mean "people"? _____

_____

3. What suffix is used to mean "full of"? _____

_____

4. What suffix is used to mean "like" or "belong to"? _____

_____

5. What is a compound word? _____

_____

6. What is meant by the contextual meaning of a word? _____

_____

_____

P: PERFECTING READING SKILLS

A. Comprehending Sentences Using Idioms

Directions. Read each sentence, and answer the questions that follow it to see if you understand the idiomatic expressions used. Idiomatic expressions are colorful, sometimes slang, ways of saying things.

1. Pablo's work is a far cry from that of his brother's.

   a. Does the sentence mean Pablo's work is better than his sister's?

   _____

   b. What does "a far cry" mean? _____

   _____

2. Look Gino, just be honest, tell them you did it, and face the music.

   a. Is Gino guilty of something? _____

   b. How do you know? _____

   _____

3. Gino is afraid he will get a raw deal if he tells them because they never liked him in the first place.

   a. What does "raw deal" mean? _____

   _____

   b. Why is Gino afraid of them? _____

   _____

4. Follow my advice, Gino, and I'll stick by you through thick and thin.

   a. Is the person talking to Gino a friend? _____

b. How do you know? _____

_____

5. Grandpa was under the weather last week, but he says he's fit as a fiddle now.

   a. What was wrong with Grandpa last week? _____

   _____

   b. Is he feeling well now? _____

6. You must learn to keep your nose to the grindstone, or you'll never get your work done.

   a. What does the sentence mean? _____

   _____

   b. What picture or image do you get in your mind when you read

   "keep your nose to the grindstone"? _____

   _____

7. Bill, will you just lay off! Going out with you is out of the question.

   a. Is Bill "bugging" someone for a date? _____

   b. Does it sound as though he will get a date with that person? _____

   c. Why? _____

   _____

8. Lee loaned Janet the money, but she skipped town and left him holding the bag.

   a. Does Janet sound like a good friend to have? _____

   b. Is it likely that Lee will get his money back? _____

9. The first day of class Curt felt like a fish out of water.

   a. Does the sentence mean Curt was taking swimming lessons?

_____

   b. Did Curt like the first day of class? _____

   c. How do you know? _____

_____

10. My son monkeyed around with something under the hood, and the engine started right up.

   a. What was the son doing? _____

_____

   b. Does it seem that the son knew what he was doing? _____

_____

   c. How do you know? _____

_____

11. Use a little elbow grease, and the dirt will come off.

   a. Does the sentence mean you should use grease to get rid of dirt?

_____

   b. What does the sentence mean? _____

_____

_____

Discuss your answers in class.

B. Comprehending Paragraphs

Directions. Read each of the following paragraphs, and answer the questions.

1. When Henry Aaron was young, he got a job delivering ice. In those days, most people had iceboxes instead of electric refrigerators. A block of ice was kept in the icebox to keep food cool. Henry's job was to

mark off a piece of ice the size the customer needed. With a sharp-pointed ice pick, he chopped the piece from a big cake of ice. Usually, the chopped pieces of ice were from twenty-five to fifty pounds. Henry had to carry these blocks of ice from the truck to the customer's icebox. This job may have helped Henry develop his strong wrists that later would bat more home runs than anyone else.

a. Whom is the paragraph about? _____

_____

b. When did the events in the paragraph take place? _____

_____

c. What is the paragraph about? _____

_____

_____

_____

2. When Hank Aaron was eighteen years old, he signed a contract with the Milwaukee Brave C Team. That was in 1952. It was a tough period in his life. It was the first time he had to stay with white people. Being from the South, he knew which places were closed to him there. But new to the North, Hank soon learned that some places where blacks were supposed to be welcome did not want him. He also discovered that some sports reporters and even some of his teammates were biased because of his color. But he stuck it out. Times got better, and so did his playing.

a. What is the paragraph about? _____

_____

_____

_____

b. What does this paragraph tell you about Hank Aaron's character?

_____

c. How would you feel and what would you do if you were in the same

Hank Aaron (Photograph: Wide World Photos)

situation Aaron was in 1952? _____

_____

_____

_____

3. On March 14, 1954, Henry Aaron received his big break. The Braves were playing against the New York Yankees. Bobby Thomson, the Braves' left fielder, got a hit. He slid into second base so hard he broke his ankle. To the surprise of everyone, Braves manager Charlie Grimm picked rookie Henry to fill in. Aaron became the regular left fielder for the Braves.

    a. What sentence in the paragraph sums up the point of the para-

       graph? _____

    b. Why was Bobby Thomson's bad break a good break for Aaron?

       _____

       _____

    c. What is a "rookie"? _____

       _____

4. Hank Aaron had a lot to learn his first season. His first few games were not too impressive. Aaron couldn't seem to get a hit. He also made some serious fielding errors. During one game, he was running to base when his hat fell off. Henry made the mistake of going back to get it! But Braves manager Grimm knew Henry was trying too hard. He had faith in Aaron. On April 23, 1954, his faith paid off. Hank hit his first major-league home run. That was the first of a record 715 home runs for Henry Aaron.

    a. Why do you suppose Braves manager Grimm had faith in Aaron?

       _____

       _____

    b. What do you think would have happened to Henry Aaron's career

       if Grimm had not had faith in him? _____

_____

_____

5. During the 1974 season, the Braves were playing the Los Angeles Dodgers. Almost 54,000 people were crowded into Atlanta Stadium. They were there to see if Henry Aaron was going to break the great Babe Ruth's home run record. The first time Aaron came to bat, the pitcher walked him. In the fourth inning, Hank was at bat again. He was thrown a fast ball. Aaron snapped his wrists. The bat hit the ball sending it over a 385 foot sign. His first swing of the game brought him his 715th home run. He broke the Babe's long-standing record.

a. Where did Aaron break the Babe's home run record? _____

_____

b. When? _____

c. Why did the pitcher walk Aaron the first time he went to bat? _____

_____

d. What was Babe Ruth's home run record? _____

_____

e. How do you think Aaron felt about his record-breaking home run?

_____

_____

_____

Discuss your answers in class.

C. Comprehending This Chapter

Directions. As a review of this chapter, discuss these questions in class. Your instructor may want you to write answers to some of the questions.

1. What words at the beginning of the chapter (p. 130) do you need to review?
2. What are homonyms? Name at least six pairs of homonyms.

3. What can the prefix *in* mean? Name at least four words using the prefix *in*.
4. What do the following suffixes mean? *ish; er* and *or; ful; able* and *ible*. Give some examples of words using these suffixes.
5. What are compound words? Give at least five examples.
6. What comprehension problems, if any, did you have in the last two drills?
7. What do you feel you have learned or relearned from this chapter?

CHAPTER 6

Objectives

P: PREREADING DRILLS

A. Words to Know
B. Warm-up Drills

R: READING DRILL

A. Reading and Thinking About What You Read
"The Butchering at Wounded Knee" by Black Elk
as told to John Neihardt.
B. Comprehension Check

E: EXERCISES IN VOCABULARY

A. Drills
1: Words Often Confused
2: Prefixes
3: Suffixes
4: Compound Words
5: Words in Context
B. Vocabulary Check

P: PERFECTING READING SKILLS

A. Comprehending Sentences
B. Comprehending Paragraphs
C. Comprehending This Chapter

OBJECTIVES

When you have finished with this chapter you will

1. Recognize and be able to use at least 90 percent of the vocabulary words listed in the "Words to Know" section.

2. Have learned or reviewed at least thirty words that are often confused, such as *accept* and *except*, *breath* and *breathe*, and *decent* and *descent*.

3. Know the definitions of the prefixes *pre*, *de*, *dis*, and *re*.

4. Know how to use the suffixes *al*, *ive*, *ment*, *est*, *er*, and *ous*.

5. Know how to use compound words to shorten phrases and sentences.

6. Know how to use various context clues to define unfamiliar words.

7. Have developed your reading comprehension skills in recognizing main ideas, drawing inferences, comparing and contrasting, and interpreting what you read.

P: PREREADING DRILLS

A. Words to Know

Directions. Read the following words aloud. Study the definitions and sample sentences.

1. *sacred* — holy, blessed, divine, worshiped.

   Black Elk wore his sacred shirt only when he went into battle.

2. *Wasichu* — an Indian term that refers to the white man (but does not refer to skin color).

   The Wasichu soldiers rode over the hill in scattered formation.

3. *gulch* — a small, narrow, deep-sided valley; a gap between hills; an arroyo; a ravine.

   The women and children ran into the gulch to hide from the soldiers.

4. *stunted* — having had one's growth stopped; not able to grow.

   They also hid behind the stunted pine trees, hoping not to be seen.

5. *ridge* — the top or upper part, especially when the top is long and narrow.

   The cavalry rode along the mountain ridge.

6. *scatter* — to break up; to divide; to separate.

   When the Wasichu cavalrymen rode into the gulch, they scattered the Indian women and children.

7. *gulley* — a small dry gulch, usually a place cut out by once running water.

   The gulley behind the stunted pines is a safe place to hide.

8. *huddle* — to stoop low and keep arms and legs close to the body.

   She was huddled in the corner, almost frightened to death.

9. *vision* — a prophecy; an unusual mental experience where one becomes aware of something through some divine or unexplained way.

   When Curly was young, he had a vision that caused him to change his name to Crazy Horse.

10. *revenge* — getting back at someone; punishment in order to get even.

When Black Elk saw the children murdered, he wanted to seek revenge on the soldiers.

11. *wrestle*—to struggle at close quarters; tussle; grapple.

    The Indian tried to wrestle the gun from the soldier's hands.

12. *butchering*—the act of killing without mercy or concern.

    The butchering of Indians at Wounded Knee in 1890 is a disgrace this country still bears.

13. *heaped*—thrown in a pile.

    The dead bodies were heaped into the gulley.

B. Warm-up Drills

Drill 1

Directions. Select the correct word from the list you just studied, and write it in the blanks in the sentences below. You may need to add a letter or letters to the word from the list to make it fit the sentence, such as *ed* to make the word past tense.

1. I carried with me only the sacred bow I had seen in my _____

    _____.

2. Just south of the burying ground on the little hill, a deep, dry _____

    _____ runs nearly to the top of the ridge.

3. The baby's growth will be _____ if she doesn't get the proper food.

4. The women and children were _____ under a clay bank.

5. In my vision, I knew I must make a _____ shirt and bow before going to battle.

6. Black Elk rode over the _____ of the mountain and down into a ravine.

7. Their bodies were in a _____ because they had huddled together.

8. All the young warriors wanted to take _____ on the soldiers.

9. The Sioux hated the _____ soldiers.

10. The two of them _____ over the rifle.

Check your answers with these:
1. vision, 2. gulch (or gulley), 3. stunted, 4. huddled, 5. sacred,
6. ridge, 7. heap, 8. revenge, 9. Wasichu, 10. wrestled.

Drill 2

Directions. Move your eyes quickly from left to right. Mark the word by the number every time it appears on the same line. Don't look back on a line. Don't change mistakes. Work rapidly. Try to finish in thirty seconds or less.

Begin timing.

1. soldier	sold	solder	soldier	solid	soldier
2. shoulder	should	shoulder	shudder	should	shoulder
3. protect	protected	protecting	protect	protected	protects
4. flaming	farming	flaming	flame	flamed	flaming
5. wrist	waist	write	wrist	waist	wrist
6. breast	beast	breast	beast	breast	beast
7. courage	courage	courageous	courage	cougar	court
8. church	chance	churned	church	church	chunk
9. cannon	canon	canon	cannon	canon	cannon
10. stack	stack	stock	stack	stock	stock
11. shawl	shame	shawl	shame	shame	shawl
12. surround	surround	surrounds	surround	surrounds	
13. whipped	whopped	whipped	wiped	whopped	whipped
14. adopted	adapted	adopted	adapted	adopted	adopted
15. charged	charged	changed	charged	changed	changed

TIME: _____

Check each line to see if you marked the correct word every time it appears. Make sure you know all the words in the drill. The words by the numbers appear in the article in this chapter.

TOTAL LINES CORRECT: _____

Drill 3

Directions. Follow the same directions as in the last drill. Try to finish in thirty seconds or less.
Begin timing.

1. sacred	scarred scar sacred scarred sacred
2. gulch	gulley gulch gulley gulch gulley
3. stunted	stunned stunned stunted stunted stunned
4. vision	version visual visor vision vision
5. scatter	scamper scatter scatter scamper scamper
6. ridge	bridge rid bridge ridge ridges ridge
7. revenge	revenge avenge reverse revenge avenge
8. wrestle	whistle wrists wrestle wrest wrestle
9. butcher	blotter butch bunches butcher batches
10. relatives	relatives relates relatives relativity relates
11. meant	means mean meant meat meant
12. enough	enough enormous evenly enough another
13. shining	shines shinney shining shinney shinning
14. gallop	gallant gallop gallant gallop gallons
15. monument	manual moment monument memorial

TIME: _____

Check each line carefully for mistakes. Learn any words you are not sure about. All the words by the numbers appear in the following article.

TOTAL LINES CORRECT: _____

R: READING DRILL

A. Reading and Thinking About What You Read

Directions. The article you are about to read is from the book *Black Elk Speaks*. Black Elk was a respected holy man of the Oglala Sioux. His people lived in the lands now known as the Dakotas. Look below at the title of the part of the book you are going to read. Now answer these questions.

1. What do you think Wounded Knee is? _____

   _____

2. Based on the title, what do you think the article will be about? _____

   _____

3. Does the title make it sound as though the article will be funny or

   serious? _____ Why? _____

   _____

Now read the article, and answer the questions as you come to them.

THE BUTCHERING AT WOUNDED KNEE
Black Elk as told to John G. Neihardt

[1] I started out alone on the old road that ran across the hills to Wounded Knee. I had no gun. I carried only the sacred bow of the west that I had seen in my great vision. I had gone only a little way when a band of young men came galloping after me. The first two who came up were Loves War and Iron Wasichu. I asked what they were going to do, and they said they were just going to see where the shooting was. Then the others were coming up, and some older men.

From *Black Elk Speaks* by John G. Neihardt, copyright by John G. Neihardt, published by Simon & Schuster Pocket Books.

Big Foot dead at Wounded Knee (Photograph: The Bettmann Archive, Inc.)

[2] We rode fast, and there were about twenty of us now. The shooting was getting louder. A horseback from over there came galloping very fast toward us, and he said: "Hey-hey-hey! They have murdered them!" Then he whipped his horse and rode away faster toward Pine Ridge.

1. Where is Black Elk going? _____

_____

2. What do you think is going on at this point in the story? _____

_____

3. What do you think they are going to find when the Indians get where

they're going? _____

_____

[3] In a little while we had come to the top of the ridge where, looking to the east, you can see for the first time the monument and the burying ground on the little hill where the church is. That is where the terrible thing started. Just south of the burying ground on the little hill a deep dry gulch runs about east and west, very crooked, and it rises westward to nearly the top of the ridge where we were. It had no name, but the Wasichus sometimes call it Battle Creek now. We stopped on the ridge not far from the head of the dry gulch. Wagon guns [cannon] were still going off over there on the little hill, and they were going off again where they hit along the gulch. There was much shooting down yonder, and there were many cries, and we could see cavalrymen scattered over the hills ahead of us. Cavalrymen were riding along the gulch and shooting into it, where the women and children were running away and trying to hide in the gullies and the stunted pines.
[4] A little way ahead of us, just below the head of the dry gulch, there were some women and children who were huddled under a clay bank, and some cavalrymen were there pointing guns at them.

4. How do you think Black Elk felt when he saw the soldiers pointing

guns at the Indian women and children? _____

_____

5. What do you think will happen next? _____

_____

[5] We stopped back behind the ridge, and I said to the others: "Take courage. These are our relatives. We will try to get them back." Then we all sang a song which went like this:

"A thunder being nation I am, I have said.
A thunder being nation I am, I have said.
You shall live.
You shall live.
You shall live.
You shall live."

[6] Then I rode over the ridge and the others after me, and we were crying: "Take courage! It is time to fight!" The soldiers who were guarding our relatives shot at us and then ran away fast, and some more cavalrymen on the other side of the gulch did too. We got our relatives and sent them across the ridge to the northwest where they would be safe.

[7] I had no gun, and when we were charging, I just held the sacred bow out in front of me with my right hand. The bullets did not hit us at all.

[8] We found a little baby lying all alone near the head of the gulch. I could not pick her up just then, but I got her later and some of my people adopted her. I just wrapped her up tighter in a shawl that was around her and left her there. It was a safe place, and I had other work to do.

6. What "other work" does Black Elk have to do? _____ _____

_____

_____

[9] The soldiers had run eastward over the hills where there were some more soldiers, and they were off their horses and lying down. I told the others to stay back, and I charged upon them holding the sacred bow out toward them with my right hand. They all shot at me, and I could hear bullets all around me, but I ran my horse right close to them, and then swung around. Some soldiers across the gulch began shooting at me too, but I got back to the others and was not hurt at all.

[10] By now many other Lakotas, who had heard the shooting, were coming up from Pine Ridge, and we all charged on the soldiers. They ran eastward toward where the trouble began. We followed down along the dry gulch, and what we saw was terrible. Dead and wounded women and children and little babies were scattered all along there where they had been trying to run away. The soldiers had followed along the gulch, as they ran, and murdered them in there. Sometimes they were in heaps

because they had huddled together, and some were scattered all along. Sometimes bunches of them had been killed and torn to pieces where the wagon guns hit them. I saw a little baby trying to suck its mother, but she was bloody and dead.

[11] There were two little boys at one place in this gulch. They had guns and they had been killing soldiers all by themselves. We could see the soldiers they had killed. The boys were all alone there, and they were not hurt. These were very brave little boys.

7. Why do you think the soldiers were killing women and children? _____

_____

[12] When we drove the soldiers back, they dug themselves in, and we were not enough people to drive them out from there. In the evening they marched off up Wounded Knee Creek, and then we saw all that they had done there.

[13] Men and women and children were heaped and scattered all over the flat at the bottom of the little hill where the soldiers had their wagon-guns, and westward up the dry gulch all the way to the high ridge, the dead women and children and babies were scattered.

[14] When I saw this I wished that I had died too, but I was not sorry for the women and children. It was better for them to be happy in the other world, and I wanted to be there too. But before I went there I wanted to have revenge. I thought there might be a day, and we should have revenge.

[15] After the soldiers marched away, I heard from my friend, Dog Chief, how the trouble started, and he was right there by Yellow Bird when it happened. This is the way it was:

8. Why is what is about to be told important to understanding what you

have already read? _____

_____

_____

[16] In the morning the soldiers began to take all the guns away from the Big Foots, who were camped in the flat below the little hill where the monument and burying ground are now. The people had stacked most of their guns, and even their knives, by the tepee where Big Foot was lying sick. Soldiers were on the little hill and all around, and there were soldiers across the dry gulch to the south and over east along Wounded Knee Creek too. The people were nearly surrounded, and the wagon-guns were pointing at them.

[17] Some had not yet given up their guns, and so the soldiers were searching all the tepees, throwing things around and poking into everything. There was a man called Yellow Bird, and he and another man were standing in front of the tepee where Big Foot was lying sick. They had white sheets around and over them, with eyeholes to look through, and they had guns under these. An officer came to search them. He took the other man's gun, and then started to take Yellow Bird's. But Yellow Bird would not let go. He wrestled with the officer, and while they were wrestling, the gun went off and killed the officer. Wasichus and some others have said he meant to do this, but Dog Chief was standing right there, and he told me it was not so. As soon as the gun went off, Dog Chief told me, an officer shot and killed Big Foot who was lying sick inside the tepee.

[18] Then suddenly nobody knew what was happening, except that the soldiers were all shooting and the wagon-guns began going off right in among the people.

[19] Many were shot down right there. The women and children ran into the gulch and up west, dropping all the time, for the soldiers shot them as they ran. There were only about a hundred warriors and there were nearly five hundred soldiers. The warriors rushed to where they had piled their guns and knives. They fought soldiers with only their hands until they got their guns.

[20] Dog Chief saw Yellow Bird run into a tepee with his gun, and from there he killed soldiers until the tepee caught fire. Then he died full of bullets.

[21] It was a good winter day when all this happened. The sun was shining. But after the soldiers marched away from their dirty work, a heavy snow began to fall. The wind came up in the night. There was a big blizzard, and it grew very cold. The snow drifted deep in the crooked gulch, and it was one long grave of butchered women and children and babies, who had never done any harm and were only trying to run away.

9. What is your reaction to this true story? _____

_____

_____

B. Comprehension Check

Directions. Answer the following questions without looking back at the article.

Recall

1. What weapon did Black Elk take into battle? _____

_____

2. T or F.   Black Elk was sorry for the dead women and children.
3. T or F.   The soldiers were searching the Indians for guns when the trouble started.
4. T or F.   There were about 500 soldiers and only 100 Indian warriors.

Interpretation

5. Do you think Black Elk's sacred bow kept him from being hit by the soldiers' bullets? _____ Why? _____

_____

6. If Yellow Bird had given up his gun when the soldiers wanted it, do you think the fight would not have happened? _____ Why? _____

_____

_____

7. Why do you think the Indians called cannons "wagon-guns"? _____

_____

_____

Application

8. Pretend you are a judge. Whose side do you think you would favor if you had to decide who started the fighting? _____ Why? _____

_____

_____

9. Do you think people will ever quit killing each other? _____

   Why? _____

   _____

   _____

E: EXERCISES IN VOCABULARY

A: Drills

Drill 1: Words Often Confused

Directions. Below are some sentences. Below each sentence are words that are often confused or misused. Write the correct word in the blank.

1. Marlon Brando was not there to _____ his Academy Award.

   accept (ăk-sĕpt′) except (ĕk-sĕpt′)

2. The smoke was so thick we could hardly _____.

   breath (brĕth) breathe (brēth)

3. The diver cut herself on the _____ while looking for pearls.

   coral (kor′əl) corral (kə-ral′)

4. We all watched as the hang glider made its _____ toward us.

   decent (dēs′ənt) descent (dĭ-sent′)

5. The blankets they gave the Indians had been used by _____

   _____ persons as they, too, became sick.

   diseased (di-zēzd′) deceased (di-sēst′)

6. The court _____ will probably last for weeks.

   trial (trī′əl) trail (trāl)

7. Hitler's _____ did not last very long.

   empire (ĕm′-pīr) umpire (ŭm-pīr)

8. Sadie grew up to be _____ the young lady.

   quiet (kwī′ĭt) quite (kwīt) quit (kwīt)

9. _____ going to be a nice day.

   Its (ĭts) It's (ĭts)

10. The shirt was too _____, so he returned it.

   lose (lo͞oz) loose (lo͞os)

11. Everyone may leave _____ you, John.

   accept (ăk sĕpt') except (ĕk-sĕpt')

12. Let me catch my _____.

   breath (brĕth) breathe (brēth)

13. He seems like a _____ guy.

   descent (di-sent') decent (dēs'ənt)

14. Lillie has tried very hard to _____ smoking.

   quite (kwīt) quit (kwĭt)

15. Don't _____ that book; _____
    the only copy I have.

   loose (lo͞os)   its (ĭts)

   lose (lo͞oz)   it's (its)

Check your answers with these:
1. accept, 2. breathe, 3. coral, 4. descent, 5. diseased, 6. trial,
7. empire, 8. quite, 9. It's (It is), 10. loose, 11. except, 12. breath,
13. decent, 14. quit, 15. lose, it's (it is).

Drill 2: Prefixes

Directions. Below are some more prefixes you should learn. Use them to
fill in the blanks in front of the following words. Some words may take
more than one prefix.

pre = before   *dis* = no longer
de = down, away   *re* = repeat, do again

1. ____ view	11. ____ planning
2. ____ own	12. ____ able
3. ____ fix	13. ____ open
4. ____ grade	14. ____ agree
5. ____ paid	15. ____ throne
6. ____ appear	16. ____ fresh
7. ____ feat	17. ____ form
8. ____ do	18. ____ lay
9. ____ caution	19. ____ like
10. ____ allow	20. ____ code

Check your answers with these:
1. preview, 2. disown, 3. prefix, 4. degrade, 5. prepaid, 6. disappear *or* reappear, 7. defeat, 8. redo, 9. precaution, 10. disallow, 11. preplanning, 12. disable, 13. reopen, 14. disagree, 15. dethrone, 16. refresh, 17. reform, 18. delay *or* relay, 19. dislike, 20. decode.

Drill 3: Suffixes

Directions. Below are some more suffixes you should know. Use them to fill in the blanks behind the following words. Some words may take more than one suffix.

-al	-ment	-er
-ive	-est	-ous

1. act _____	6. protect _____
2. music _____	7. content _____
3. light _____	8. poison _____
4. move _____	9. select _____
5. clean _____	10. renew _____

11. enormous _____   16. murder _____

12. treat _____   17. near _____

13. electric _____   18. impress _____

14. strong _____   19. politic _____

15. assign _____   20. agree _____

Check your answers with these:
1. active, 2. musical, 3. lighter, lightest, 4. movement, 5. cleaner, cleanest, 6. protective, 7. contentment, 8. poisonous, 9. selective, 10. renewal, 11. enormously, 12. treatment, 13. electrical, 14. stronger, strongest, 15. assignment, 16. murderous, 17. nearer, nearest, 18. impressive, 19. political, 20. agreement.

Drill 4: Compound Words

Directions. Read the following sentences. In the blank that follows the sentence, write in a compound word that could be used in place of the part of the sentence that is underlined. For example:

The light of the moon was shining in the window. *moonlight*

1. Make a ball of snow, and throw it at your sister. _____

2. Mom is decorating my bedroom with some pretty paper that goes on the walls. _____

3. On her day of birth, Jeanne will be twenty-five years old.

_____

4. When that tree is grown to its full size, it will be about thirty feet high. _____

5. The Indians cut holes for their eyes in the sheets. _____

6. The boss thinks he'll make a good hand with the cows.

_____

7. When the men in the cavalry rode up the hill, they were met by the

   Indians. _____

8. The walking place along the side of the road was almost covered with

   weeds. _____

9. Tell Jerry, the boy who brings the newspaper, to stop delivery until

   we come back from vacation. _____

10. The room where we have school needs cleaning. _____

Drill 5: Words in Context

Directions. Below are some sentences. In each sentence there is an underlined word. See if you can figure out what the underlined word means by the way it is used in context. Write your answers in the blanks.

1. The jeweler appraised the diamond necklace at $60,000.

   _____

2. My friends seemed incredulous and laughed when I told them I had

   seen a flying saucer.

   _____

3. The police were unable to elicit the truth from the criminal.

   _____

4. A dirge was sung at the man's burial.

   _____

5. Mary will not be underline{eligible} for graduate school unless she passes her Chemistry III class.

_____

6. Ellen made several underline{vain} attempts to stop smoking.

_____

7. When we ran out of food, we began to look for some underline{edible} berries.

_____

8. They need to underline{dredge} the mouth of the harbor because boats can't get through.

_____

9. The lake was so underline{placid} it looked as though you could walk on the water.

_____

10. Gasoline is highly underline{flammable} and should be used with care.

_____

Check your answers with these. Your wording may be different. 1. gave value to; checked its worth, 2. unbelieving; hard to accept or believe, 3. to get *or* bring out, 4. a song for the dead; a funeral song, 5. qualified; able, 6. unsuccessful, 7. able to eat, 8. to dig out, 9. peaceful; calm; flat, 10. able to catch fire or explode easily.

B. Vocabulary Check

Part A

Directions. Below are some pronunciation key spellings of words in this chapter. In the blank, write what the word is.

1. brēth _____

2. ăk-sĕpt′ _____

3. lōoz _____

4. kwī′-ĭt _____

5. dēs′ənt _____

6. trī′əl _____

7. kwĭt _____

8. lōos _____

9. di sēst′ _____

10. kor′əl _____

Part B

Directions. Circle the prefixes in the following words.

1. preschool
2. insert
3. deflate
4. remove
5. prepaid

6. relearn
7. degrade
8. disown
9. remain
10. disband

11. deform
12. pretend
13. report
14. disarm
15. defeat

Part C

Directions. Write the correct suffix for the underlined word in each sentence below.

1. My grandmother is very act_____ for her age.

2. Sally has music_____ talents that should be developed.

3. This box is light_____ than that one.

4. The contents of the bottle are very poison_____ .

5. Be more select_____ the next time you buy a car.

6. The electric_____ shock almost killed him.

7. Bill's service record is very impress_____ .

8. How many assign _____ did you complete.

9. Willie proved he is the strong _____ of all of them.

10. When is the renew _____ date on your driver's license?

Part D

Directions. Draw a line between the words that make up the following compound words.

1. inside	3. rainbow	5. daybreak	7. cavalrymen
2. sometimes	4. buckskin	6. outstretched	8. horseback

Part E

Directions. Write a sentence correctly using each of the following words. You may add suffixes if you need to.

1. appraise: _____

_____

2. vain: _____

_____

3. elicit: _____

_____

4. edible: _____

_____

5. placid: _____

_____

P: PERFECTING READING SKILLS

A. Comprehending Sentences

Directions. Read each sentence, and answer the questions that follow. Try not to use the words in the sentences when you write your answers.

1. The ownership of the company will change hands next month unless the present owners come up with the money.

    a. What might happen next month? _____

    _____

    b. Why? _____

    _____

2. We could probably buy the company for a song, and then we'd be in clover.

    a. Does the sentence imply the company is in financial trouble? _____

    _____

    b. Does it sound as though the business is a good one? _____

    Why? _____

    _____

3. Get in touch with a lawyer, Mort; you've been given a raw deal.

    a. What is Mort being told to do? _____

    _____

    b. Why? _____

    _____

4. If Tom hadn't put his foot down in the nick of time, you would be left holding the bag.

   a. What did Tom do? _____

      _____

   b. What would have happened if Tom had not done what he did?

      _____

5. After our date last week, Ed has been giving me the cold shoulder.

   a. Did Ed probably have a good time on his date? _____

   b. Why? _____

      _____

6. The way Ed treats Joan makes my blood boil; I'd love to give him a piece of my mind.

   a. How does Ed treat Joan? _____

      _____

   b. How do you know? _____

      _____

7. Look, Ed and Joe are supposed to be bosom friends; Ed didn't need to bite his head off like that!

   a. What is the relationship between Ed and Joe? _____

      _____

   b. Did Ed kill Joe? _____

   c. How do you know? _____

      _____

8. Men, leave no stone unturned; I want the killer found.

   a. What are the men supposed to do? _____

b. Where are they supposed to look? _____

_____

Discuss your answers in class.

B. Comprehending Paragraphs

Directions. Read the following paragraphs, and answer the questions that follow.

1. Some historians say that the end of the Plains Indians occurred at Wounded Knee Creek, South Dakota. In December 1890, soldiers had gathered the Sioux Indians in order to take their guns from them. Most of the Indians stacked their guns as they were told to do. But when one Indian refused, shooting started. It suddenly got out of hand. When the shooting stopped, over 300 Indians, mostly women and children, had been senselessly killed. After this, there were no more major Indian wars in the plains areas.

   a. What is the main idea of this paragraph? _____

   _____

   b. What is meant by the phrase "end of the Plains Indians"? _____

   _____

   _____

   _____

   c. How does this version of the Wounded Knee killings compare with

   Black Elk's story? _____

   _____

   _____

2. When he was young, Curly had a vision. He dreamed and went into the world where there is nothing but the spirits of all things. He was on his horse in that vision. The horse, himself, the trees, the grass,

the stones—everything was made of spirit. Nothing was hard. Everything seemed to float. His horse was standing there. Yet it danced around like a horse made only of shadow. That is how Curly got his name, Crazy Horse. It does not mean that his horse was crazy or wild, but that in his vision the horse danced around in a strange way.

    a. What is the main idea of the paragraph? _____

    _____

    _____

    b. Do you believe there is a "world where there is nothing but the

    spirits of all things"? _____

    _____

    _____

    c. Can you guess how many Indians got their names? _____

    _____

    _____

3. Crazy Horse had many followers because of his vision and his belief that he could not be killed in battle. Though not an official chief, his followers loved him because he was concerned with his people and not with gaining wealth. He refused to accept many gifts or to own many horses, a sign of wealth. He often went without food when it was scarce. When he went into a fight, he always put himself in danger. He was never wounded in battle.

    a. What is the main idea of the paragraph? _____

    _____

    _____

    b. What is an Indian's idea of wealth? _____

    _____

    c. Plains Indians believed strongly in visions. Do you? _____

Zuñi Indian kachina dolls

Why? _____

_____

_____

4. The white man's desire for land and gold was to destroy still another Indian life-style. In 1863, the Nez Percé signed a treaty. But the Indians did not really understand the treaty they signed because it took away three-fourths of their land. The treaty left them with only a small reservation in Idaho. Confused, some of the Indians refused to

leave their homes. In 1873, they asked President Grant if they could stay. He let them stay, but two years later he changed his mind. The reason is that too many white settlers and businessmen were putting pressure on Grant for the land. In 1877, he sent an army to move the Indians to a reservation.

a. Whom is this paragraph about? _____

_____

b. Where did the events take place? _____

_____

c. What is the main idea of the paragraph? _____

_____

_____

d. How would you feel if you were told you must leave your home and

go live where the government said you will? _____

_____

_____

5. The Nez Percé peacefully started toward the reservation area. Their leader was a great man named Chief Joseph. One night during the move, some angry Indians killed eleven white men. The army out-numbered the Nez Percé two to one. When they learned of the murder of the whites, the army attacked the Indians. Chief Joseph and his small band managed to kill one-third of the soldiers and escaped into the mountains. Chief Joseph led his people over 1,300 miles trying to escape to Canada. Battles were constant during the long march. For months, Chief Joseph and fewer then 300 warriors and 400 women and children kept the entire Northwest army on the move. Finally, Chief Joseph accepted a truce offering. But he was tricked and learned, as many Indians did, that the white soldier was not to be trusted.

a. What is the main idea of the paragraph? _____

_____

b. What do you think of Chief Joseph? _____

c. Is the author of the paragraph on the side of the whites or the Indians in this report? _____ How do you know? _____

C. Comprehending This Chapter

Directions. As a review of this chapter, discuss these questions in class. Your instructor may ask you to write answers to one or more of these questions.

1. What words at the beginning of this chapter (p. 163) do you need to review?
2. Name at least five pairs of words that are often confused.
3. What do the following prefixes usually mean: *pre, de, dis, re?*
4. Name at least two words using each of the following suffixes: *al, ive, ment, est, er, ous.*
5. What are compound words? Name at least five examples.
6. What is meant by "words in context"?
7. Discuss any comprehension problems you may have had in the last two drills.
8. What did you learn or relearn by working in this chapter?

UNIT 2
CHECK TEST (Chapters 4–6)

Part 1: Word Knowledge

A. *Directions.* Underline the root word in each word listed below.

1. unartistic
2. independent
3. accountable
4. uncreative
5. realistic
6. unsocial

B. *Directions.* Circle the prefixes in the words below, and define the meaning of the words in the blank. Try not to use the root word in your definition.

7. impersonal: _____

8. inactive: _____

9. disable: _____

10. preview: _____

11. redo: _____

12. uncommon: _____

13. irreplaceable: _____

14. disapprove: _____

C. *Directions.* Circle the suffixes in the words below, and define the meaning of the word in the blank.

15. painful: _____

16. careless: _____

17. securely: _____

18. foolish: _____

19. responsible: _____

20. dependable: _____

D. *Directions.* Write in the blanks below five examples of compound words.

21. _____   24. _____

22. _____   25. _____

23. _____

Part 2: Word Usage

Directions. Below are two columns. In the blank by the word in the first column, write in the letter of the definition from the second column.

1. _____ vocational   a. to walk with self-importance

2. _____ conventional   b. sore, touchy

3. _____ sensitive   c. grapple, tussle

4. _____ practical   d. sides, points, parts

5. _____ confident   e. not able to grow

6. _____ aspects   f. relating to jobs, careers

7. _____ trot   g. a small, dry gulch

8. _____ swagger   h. jog, hurry

9. _____ lunge   i. a manner that attracts

10. _____ charisma   j. common, ordinary

11. _____ stunted   k. stoop low, crouch

12. _____ vision   l. move forward suddenly

13. _____ wrestle   m. workable, attainable

14. _____ huddle   n. a prophecy

15. _____ gulley   o. sure, certain

Part 3: Reading Comprehension

Directions. Read the two passages below, and answer the questions that follow each passage. You will have no more than twenty minutes to do this.

[1] Much research has been done on note-taking methods. Here is one method most researchers seem to agree is best for courses where the lecture and textbook readings are related. First, use 8½-by-11-inch notebook paper. That's regular notebook size. Second, only write on one side of the page. It may seem wasteful, but it isn't when it's helpful to your learning. If you write on both sides of a page, you can't spread your notes out side-by-side for review study purposes. Third, use a ruler and divide the page as follows. Make a line about two inches up from the bottom of the page all the way across. Next, about two inches from the left make a line down from the top of the page to the bottom line you drew. Then draw two lines down the page, one three inches from the two-inch line and the other three inches from that. You will then have three columns. The two-inch column on the left is for adding key phrases or changing your notes when you look them over after class. The second column (the middle one) is for your lecture notes. The last column is for your textbook reading notes. The space at the bottom is for your own thoughts, questions for the instructor, or references. If you are taking a course where the lecture and textbook readings are different, then use one notebook page for lecture notes and another for textbook notes.

1. What is the main idea of the passage? _____

_____

_____

_____

2. What is the difference between taking notes for a course where the lecture and textbook are related and a course where they are different? _____

_____

_____

_____

3. In the space below, follow the directions given in the passage and draw the lines on the following sample notebook page.

4. What use is the space at the bottom of the page? _____

_____

_____

5. How are each of the three columns to be used for note-taking? _____

_____

_____

_____   _____

[2] Here's how to take notes. The second column is for lecture notes. Learn to abbreviate words so that you aren't writing such words as *psychology*, but *psych*, & for *and*, or *g* for *ing* word endings. Also, don't try to write everything being said in lecture. Listen for key words such as *first, second, next,* or *in summary*. Good notes don't require as much writing as they do good listening and then jotting down words or phrases that will trigger your memory later. When you take notes from reading your textbook assignments, try to use your own words. Copying from the book doesn't force you to put what you've read in your own words, an important key to learning.

[3] The first column is important after the class is over. Read over your notes. Then correct or add to your notes in that first column. You may wish to use that first column to put down key words or phrases that will be useful when you review your notes before a test. Let's say today's lecture in history was on the causes of the Civil War. Your notes may contain five causes discussed in class. That first column could be used to write in "5 causes of Civil War." Later, when you review your notes before a test, that phrase will draw your attention. You would then read your notes to review the five causes of the war. If the lectures have been going along with the textbook readings, your notes in the right-hand column will deal with the causes of the Civil War as discussed in the book. All your notes will be handy for review.

[4] It is suggested that you study this way. Take your notes and cover up everything but the left-hand column. See if the clue phrases mean anything to you. For instance, after three or four weeks, will you be able to name the five causes of the Civil War? Try. If you can't remember them all, uncover your notes and review. By writing only on one side of the page, you can spread your notes out and place them in any order you want for study purposes.

6. What is the main idea of the passage? _____

_____

_____

_____

7. Why is it important to learn to use abbreviations when taking

lecture notes? _____

_____

_____

UNIT 3

CHAPTER 7

Objectives

P: PREREADING DRILLS

 A. Words to Know
 B. Warm-up Drills

R: READING DRILL

 A. Reading and Thinking About What You Read
   "Puff, Puff, Puff That Cigarette!"
 B. Comprehension Check

E: EXERCISES IN VOCABULARY

 A. Drills
   1: Synonyms
   2: Antonyms
   3: Using the Correct Word
   4: Word Formation
 B. Vocabulary Check

P: PERFECTING READING SKILLS

 A. Comprehending Paragraphs
 B. Comprehending Short Essays: "Big Business: Selling Cancer"
 C. Comprehending This Chapter

OBJECTIVES

When you have finished with this chapter, you will

1. Recognize and be able to use at least 90 percent of the vocabulary words in the "Words to Know" section.

2. Know what synonyms are.

3. Know what antonyms are.

4. Know and be able to use at least fifty synonyms and antonyms used in this chapter.

5. Know how to change words to form different parts of speech, such as verbs to nouns, nouns to adjectives, and so on.

6. Have developed your reading comprehension skills in recognizing main ideas, cause-effect relationships, and an author's bias.

7. Have developed your ability to carry on class discussions about what you have read.

P: PREREADING DRILLS

A. Words to Know

Directions. Read the following words aloud. Make sure you know their meanings. All the words appear in the essay you will read in this chapter.

1. *fad*—craze, style, trend, usually something accepted by most for a short time.

   The latest fad in sports right now is jogging.

2. *custom*—habit, accepted rule.

   The custom of smoking has been around a long time.

3. *fashion item*—something in style at the time.

   The latest fashion item in smoking is colored cigarettes.

4. *inhale*—to breathe in.

   Pipe smokers do not inhale their smoke.

5. *odor*—smell, aroma.

   The odor from stale cigarettes is foul.

6. *persuade*—to convince, to encourage.

   It was not easy to persuade her to try smoking.

7. *vile*—foul, nasty, disgusting, vulgar, offensive.

   To many, cigarette smoking is a vile habit.

8. *expensive*—costly, not cheap.

   Cigarette smoking can be expensive on your pocketbook and your health.

9. *survive*—to last, to continue, to pull through.

   The custom of smoking has survived centuries.

10. *tripled*—grew three times more than what originally was.

    The sales of the new cigarettes tripled in less than a year.

11. *nicotine*—colorless, oily stuff in tobacco that stimulates.

    It's the nicotine in tobacco to which smokers become addicted.

12. *blend* —a mixture, a combination of things.

   Most cigarettes are made from a blend of different tobaccos.

13. *situation* —place, position, spot, point.

   The new law, if passed, puts cigarette smokers in a bad situation.

14. *crew* —group, band, bunch, company.

   The night crew just came to work.

15. *century* —100-year period.

   Smoking has been going on in Europe for over four centuries.

B. Warm-up Drills

Drill 1

Directions. Read each sentence below. Write in the correct word from the choices under each sentence.

1. Smoking is an _____ habit to start.

   expansive   expensive

2. If you want to _____, don't inhale the fumes.

   survival   survive

3. It was hard to _____ him to see the doctor for a check-up.

   persuade   pursued

4. The juice was a _____ of three different juices.

   blender   blend

5. In the last half _____, cigarette smoking has increased.

   centuries   century

6. The _____ of the ship was to let half the crew go

   customary   custom

   ashore while the other half kept watch.

7. Everyone smelled a _____ aroma coming from the back room.

    odor   vile

8. The advertising industry creates new _____ so that we will keep spending money.

    fads   fades

9. The latest _____ item is meant to get more women to smoke.

    fasten   fashion

10. The filter is supposed to keep most of the _____ from getting in your lungs.

    tobacco   nicotine

Check your answers with these:
1. expensive, 2. survive, 3. persuade, 4. blend, 5. century, 6. custom,
7. vile, 8. fads, 9. fashion, 10. nicotine.

Drill 2

Directions. Move your eyes quickly from left to right. Mark the word by the number every time it appears on the same line. Work rapidly. Don't look back on a line, and don't change any mistakes. Try to finish in thirty-five seconds or less.

Begin timing.

1. ever	every even ever even ever every
2. though	though through though through through
3. leaves	leave leaf leaves leave leaves
4. stepped	stopped stopped stepped stopped stepped
5. ashore	ashes ashore ashame ashame ashore
6. amaze	amuse amuse amuse amaze amaze
7. brought	brought bought bought bought brought
8. chewing	chew chewed crewing chewing chewing
9. cheap	cheep cheap cheap cheap cheaply
10. fad	fade fad fad fade fade
11. expensive	expensive expansive expansion expensive
12. quit	quite quiet quit quite quiet quit
13. industry	industrial industry industrious industrial
14. blend	blond blown blend blender blended
15. crops	corpse cops crops corpse cops crops

TIME: _____

Check each line carefully. Make certain you underlined the correct word on each line. Learn any words you don't know.

TOTAL LINES CORRECT: _____

Drill 3

Directions. Follow the same directions as in the last drill. The only difference here is that you will be looking for a two-word phrase, not a single word. For example:

1. green leaves   green eyes   green leaves   green house
2. new custom   new costume   new candy   new custom

Try to finish in forty seconds or less.
Begin timing.

1. vile odor	file order vile aroma vile odor
2. curious mind	curious mink curious mind curious cat
3. dried leaves	dead leaves dried lunch dried leaves
4. not accepted	now accepted not accepted not expected
5. next crop	next corpse next cop next crop
6. tripled sales	tripled sales tripled sails tripled sales
7. published report	published book published report
8. tobacco blend	tobacco blend tobacco book tobacco crop
9. old habit	old hobby old habit old house
10. new situation	nice situation now situated new situation
11. milder taste	milky taste milder taste milder touch
12. quite vile	quit now quite mild quite vile
13. nicotine fit	nicotine fad nicotine fit nicotine time
14. cheaply made	cheap maid cheaply run cheaply made
15. brought ashore	brought home brought ashore brought

TIME: _____

Check each line carefully. Some lines may have the phrase more than once. Learn any words or phrases you don't know.

TOTAL LINES CORRECT: _____

Drill 4

Directions. Follow the same directions as in the last drill. Work quickly. Try to finish in 40 seconds or less.
Begin timing.

1. beautiful scenery   beautiful hills   beauty   beautiful scenery
2. clever situation   clever fellow   clever situation   clever mind
3. even desirable   every desire   even decide   even desirable
4. probably due   probably dew   probably due   probably do
5. some smoke   some smoke   some stuff   some smokers
6. don't want   don't wait   don't want   don't waste
7. receive millions   receive much   receive   receive millions
8. cancer-causing   cancer-caused   cancer   cancer-causing
9. related to   relieved to   related two   related to
10. beat faster   beat slower   beat faster   beat fast
11. was published   was published   was perished   published
12. more cases   more causes   more cases   more causes
13. the nonsmokers   the nonsmokers   the nun smokers
14. federal taxes   federal tacks   federal tax   federal taxes
15. blood pressure   blood relative   blood pressure   block pressure

TIME: _____

Check each line for mistakes. Some lines have the phrase more than once. Learn any words you don't know.

TOTAL LINES CORRECT: _____

Drill 5

Directions. Before you go on, make certain you know all the words in the first four drills.

R: READING DRILL

A. Reading and Thinking About What You Read

Directions. Take a minute to look over the following essay. Don't read it. Just answer these questions:

1. Based on the title, what do you think the essay is about? _____

   _____

2. Write in the titles of each heading in the essay.

   1st heading: _____

   2d heading: _____

   3d heading: _____

3. Now what do you think the essay will be about? _____

   _____

   _____

   _____

4. Do you think the essay will be *for* or *against* smoking? _____

   Why? _____

   _____

   _____

Now read the article. This time there are no questions to answer in the essay.

PUFF, PUFF, PUFF THAT CIGARETTE!

[1] Who first thought of burning leaves and sucking in the smoke no one knows. But whoever it was might be surprised if alive today. The tobacco industry today is a billion dollar business. Even though there is much proof to show that smoking tobacco is harmful, more people are smoking than ever before. Why? How did smoking tobacco get to be popular? Why do people start smoking when they know it is harmful?

A Short History

[2] Smoking was not known to Europeans before Columbus arrived in the New World in 1492. But smoking seems to have been a custom among the Indians for a long time. When Columbus and his men stepped ashore, they were greeted by the natives who offered them dried leaves wrapped in palm leaves or stuffed in pipes. Columbus and his crew were amazed to see the natives inhale the smoke that had a sharp, strange odor. Strange as it seemed, the Spanish explorers soon took up the habit themselves. They called the leaves "tobacco" which is from the natives' word for pipe, *tobaco*.

[3] Returning to Spain, Columbus brought back some dried tobacco leaves and seeds. Soon the leaves of the planted seeds were used for cigar and pipe smoking. Most people made pipes of walnut shells and straw reeds. The rich had expensive pipes of wood and silver made. It became a fashion item for both men and women.

[4] When Sir Walter Raleigh, the English explorer, went to the New World, he too brought tobacco back. It is said that he persuaded Queen Elizabeth I to try smoking. But in England, the smoking fad did not catch on as fast as in Spain. Many people felt that smoking dried up a person's brain. Others said it was harmful to the body. By 1604, King James I of England called smoking a "vile and stinking custome." Still, smoking became a fad. With the fad came a demand for more tobacco.

[5] The English colony of Jamestown, Virginia, was having a hard time surviving. With the Indians' help, the colonists tried to grow tobacco. They had poor crops in the beginning. However, in 1610, John Rolfe's experiments with growing tobacco paid off. His blend of tobacco began to sell well in Europe. His tobacco had a more pleasant smell and the smoke was milder. By 1618, the small English colony was selling more tobacco than Spain and all its tobacco colonies. Tobacco became a big business and has stayed one ever since. Why? Because the people's fad became a habit that had to be fed.

Packaged cancer sticks

Cigarettes Become Popular

[6] In the nineteenth century, cigar smoking, pipe smoking, and tobacco chewing were accepted throughout the world. Cigarettes were not very popular because of the expense. Each cigarette had to be hand rolled. In 1870, a cigarette making machine was invented. Within ten years, the tobacco companies were able to produce cigarettes quickly and cheaply. With advertising, more and more people began to smoke cigarettes.

[7] It was more than the cheap price that turned people on to cigarettes. Cigarettes could be smoked more quickly and easily than cigars or pipes. Also, cigarette smoke could be inhaled for the nicotine effects, which smokers of cigars and pipes did not do. Cigarette companies spent

millions of dollars in advertising to make women and men feel that smoking cigarettes was glamorous and romantic. An ad for Lucky Strikes even said, "Reach for a Lucky instead of a sweet." Women who had weight problems began smoking cigarettes. In one year, the sales of Lucky Strikes tripled.

[8] Today, there are about 50,000,000 smokers in the United States alone. Each year, over 500 *billion* cigarettes are sold. In addition, both state and federal governments receive millions of dollars in taxes. The federal government has been receiving over two billion dollars a year in taxes on tobacco.

[9] In 1964, the U.S. Surgeon General's Advisory Committee on Smoking and Health released the findings of their study. Cigarette smoking is related to lung cancer. When the report came out, millions of people quit smoking. But in a year, smoking was up again. The habit was too hard to break.

[10] Why? Ask the smoker. But here are the facts. In just three seconds, a cigarette makes your heart beat faster. It makes your blood pressure go up. The smoke takes the place of oxygen in your blood. It leaves cancer-causing chemicals in your body. There are 15,000 new cases of mouth cancer each year. About 13,500 of these are cigar, pipe, or cigarette smokers. In addition, smokers lose 77 million work days a year more than nonsmokers.

Why People Smoke

[12] If smoking is so bad for you, then why do people begin smoking? There are many reasons. Some young people begin smoking because their parents or their friends do. Some smoke because it makes them feel adult. Others start smoking because it's the "in" thing to do. They don't want their friends to think they are "uncool." Still others begin to smoke because they are curious.

[13] But the biggest reason people begin smoking is probably due to advertising. Look at most cigarette ads. They show pretty women, handsome men, beautiful scenery, and clever situations that make cigarette smoking seem normal, even desirable. But remember, the ads want to get you to buy cigarettes. What the ads say or suggest and the truth about smoking are quite different. If the cigarette ads told you the truth, sales would drop.

[14] No matter what the reason, once people begin smoking the habit is hard to break. Even though smokers know they are slowly killing themselves, they can't seem to stop. And although warnings that smoking is harmful appear everywhere, more new people begin the habit each year.

[15] Columbus, why did you bring those dried leaves back home with you?

B. Comprehension Check

Directions. Answer the following questions without looking back.

Recall

1. Who first started smoking tobacco?

   a. the Indians

   b. Columbus

   c. the English

   d. no one knows for sure

2. Who was John Rolfe? _____

   _____

3. Name at least three reasons given for why people smoke.

   a. _____

   b. _____

   c. _____

4. What does the essay say is the major reason people smoke? _____

   _____

   _____

Interpretation

5. Why and how did the invention of the cigarette-making machine

   change the tobacco industry? _____

   _____

   _____

6. Why is advertising important to cigarette companies? _____

_____

_____

7. How is the tobacco industry good for the state and federal governments? _____

_____

_____

8. Do you think the author of the essay is for or against smoking? _____ Why? _____

_____

_____

Application

9. Do you smoke? _____ Why? _____

_____

_____

10. Do you think, with all the proof that smoking is harmful, that laws should be passed to make smoking in public illegal? _____ Why? _____

_____

_____

_____

E: EXERCISES IN VOCABULARY

A. Drills

Drill 1: Synonyms

Directions. Synonyms are words that have the same or similar meanings. Read each line below from left to right. Underline the word that means the same or nearly the same as the word by the number. For example:

    1. large   round small <u>big</u> short

Work as quickly as you can.

1. biggest — smallest shortest little largest
2. crew — group meaning students thank
3. situation — reach maid position valuable
4. blend — usual mix freedom method
5. craze — cigarette noise liberty fad
6. custom — promise pull habit correct
7. fashion — style wrong washer beside
8. aroma — several aid recall odor
9. persuade — shop convince union suppose
10. foul — catch fowl vile human
11. harmful — bad proper strong certain
12. curious — contend interested difficult crew
13. related — connected trouble actual ache
14. business — action address always work
15. expensive — around better costly article
16. beginning — apart start ancient among
17. colony — bridge apple cause group
18. amazed — surprised birth center bridge
19. stuffed — border amuse full candle
20. illegal — cheap unlawful chief engine
21. attempt — field excite force try
22. suppose — develop imagine fault dirty
23. occur — happen either contribute contain
24. sufficient — foolish dirty enough declare
25. strike — famous hit furniture courage

Drill 2: Antonyms

Directions. Antonyms are words that are opposite in meaning. *Hot* and *cold*, *hard* and *soft*, *difficult* and *easy* are antonyms. Read each line below from left to right. Underline the word that means the opposite or nearly the opposite of the word by the number. Work as quickly as you can.

1. clean — clothes   dirty   dress   drummer
2. smooth — encounter   dinner   fortunate   rough
3. early — time   late   further   gasoline
4. lose — forest   loose   find   descendants
5. never — couple   deny   electric   always
6. distant — rear   fasten   near   crack
7. sell — college   grand   buy   happy
8. peace — journey   war   piece   nearly
9. fail — succeed   market   leaves   muscle
10. past — mention   present   feature   negative
11. dangerous — health   into   safe   library   lean
12. public — hospital   private   marriage   narrow
13. cheap — mouth   intend   judge   expensive
14. remember — hole   forget   handle   ground
15. enter — leave   iron   sheets   matter
16. beautiful — however   imagine   sense   ugly
17. alive — heavy   dead   booming   noses
18. awake — sleep   jewelry   priest   another
19. drop — opposite   round   lift   opinion
20. silent — relative   noisy   return   shame
21. village — pound   presence   shade   city
22. permit — radio   prevent   question   sometimes
23. amusing — wonderous   usually   sad   wind
24. ill — well   various   therefore   supply
25. sufficient — structure   though   lacking   through

Drill 3: Using the Correct Word (Part A)

Directions. Read the sentences below, and write in the correct word from the choices below the sentence.

1. Helen bought an _____ dress.

    expense   expensive

2. What _____ have you had in using the cash register?

    instruction   instructed

3. Dress for the party is _____ .

    informally   informal

4. It looks _____ made.

    cheap   cheaply

5. His list of _____ is three pages long.

    accomplish   accomplishments

Drill 3: Using the Correct Word (Part B)

Directions. Write a sentence using each of the following words correctly.

1. permit (n.): _____

    _____

2. resent (v.): _____

    _____

3. monumental (adj.): _____

_____

4. informally (adv.): _____

_____

5. detachment (n.): _____

_____

Drill 4: Word Formation

Directions. Below are some words with the part of speech abbreviation. In the blanks at the right, write in the correct word needed to change the word by the number to other parts of speech. For example:

1. wide (adj.) *width* _____ (n.)

Use a dictionary if you need to.

1. expense (n.) _____ (adj.)

2. fry (v.) _____ (adj.)

3. survival (n.) _____ (v.)

4. desire (v.) _____ (adj.)

5. flat (adj.) _____ (v.)

6. instruct (v.) _____ (n.)

7. informal (adj.) _____ (adv.)

8. greet (v.) _____ (n.)

9. sales (n.) _____ (v.)

10. detachment (n.) _____ (v.)

11. cheap (adj.) _____ (adv.)

12. inform (v.) _____ (n.)

13. resent (v.) _____ (n.)

14. accomplishments (n.) _____ (v.)

15. exaggerate (v.) _____ (n.)

16. adopt (v.) _____ (n.)

17. monument (n.) _____ (adj.)

18. permit (v.) _____ (n.)

19. searcher (n.) _____ (v.)

20. swindler (n.) _____ (v.)

Check your answers with these: 1. expensive, 2. fried, 3. survive,
4. desirable, 5. flatten, 6. instruction; instructor, 7. informally,
8. greeting, 9. sell, 10. detach, 11. cheaply, 12. informer,
13. resentment, 14. accomplish, 15. exaggeration, 16. adopted,
17. monumental, 18. permit; permission, 19. search, 20. swindle.

B. Vocabulary Check

Part A

Directions. Read the following paragraph, and in each blank write in the word that is missing.

If smoking is so _____ for you, then why _____

people begin smoking? There _____ many reasons. Some

young _____ begin smoking because their _____

or friends do. Some _____ because it makes them _____

_____ adult. Others start smoking _____ it's the "in" thing.

They _____ want their friends to _____ they are

"uncool." Still _____ begin to smoke because _____

are curious.

But the _____ reason people begin smoking _____

_____ probably due to advertising. _____ at most cigarette

ads. _____ show pretty women, _____ men, beautiful scenery and _____ situations that make cigarette _____

_____ seem normal, even desirable.

Part B

Directions. In the blanks following each word, write a synonym, or word that means the same.

1. crew _____   6. odor _____

2. blend _____   7. persuade _____

3. fad _____   8. costly _____

4. custom _____   9. colony _____

5. fashion _____   10. amazed _____

Part C

Directions. In the blanks following each word, write an antonym, or word that means the opposite.

1. smooth _____   6. permit _____

2. peace _____   7. loose _____

3. public _____   8. lose _____

4. remember _____ 9. sufficient _____

5. ugly _____   10. amusing _____

Part D

Directions. Read each sentence below. In the blank write in the correct word by adding the proper suffix to the word in parenthesis. For example:

The major *accomplishment* of the president will be forgotten by now. (accomplish)

1. Your _____ in the mountains will be dependent upon your ability to deal with nature. (survive)

2. Please _____ that loose flap on the tent. (flat)

3. Mary seems _____ toward me because I dated her brother. (resent)

4. The _____ got away with $15,000. (swindle)

5. Doug's _____ takes time to make assignments clear. (instruct)

NAME _____ SECTION _____ DATE _____

222 E: Exercises in Vocabulary

P: PERFECTING READING SKILLS

A. Comprehending Paragraphs

Directions. Read the following paragraphs, and answer the questions that follow each.

1. Usually, you can spot smokers even when they are not smoking. The odor of smoke is on their clothes. Sometimes tiny burn holes from ashes appear on their clothing. Their fingers are usually yellow or brown from holding cigarettes. Teeth also show stains from nicotine. And some smokers have developed a "smoker's hack" or cough.

   a. What is the main idea of the paragraph? _____

   _____

   _____

   b. What word or words could be used in the first sentence to replace

   "spot smokers"? _____

   _____

   c. Could this paragraph be used in a cigarette ad? _____ Why?

   _____

   _____

   _____

2. Some smokers get what is called "hairy tongue." This is a brown or black furlike coating on the tongue. "Hairy tongue" is caused by chemicals in smoke that keep the dead cells of the tongue's surface from wearing away as they normally would. The little bumps on the tongue (papillae) grow longer than normal if you smoke. Food gets caught in the papillae and causes bad breath.

a. What is the main idea of the paragraph? _____

_____

_____

b. Why do smokers often have bad breath? _____

_____

_____

3. One of the dangers of smoking mentioned in the Surgeon General's report is lung cancer. It has been found that the lung cancer rate for smokers is ten times higher than for nonsmokers. A person who smokes a pack of cigarettes a day is twenty times more likely to die of cancer than the nonsmoker. The cancer is caused by the tar and nicotine in cigarettes. They change and destroy lung cells. The new cells that develop become cancerous. Since cancer cells grow rapidly, they destroy normal cells. Soon the cancer cells take over. They then can enter the bloodstream. The result is often damage to the liver and brain.

a. What is the main idea of the paragraph? _____

_____

_____

b. Why does smoking cigarettes cause lung cancer? _____

_____

_____

_____

_____

c. Do you believe the information in this paragraph? _____

Why? _____

_____

_____

4. Smoking also is dangerous to your circulatory system. Your circulatory system is made up of your heart, arteries, and veins. Your heart is a muscle that pumps blood through your body. The blood that flows through your arteries brings food and oxygen to all the cells in the body. The veins carry away the cell's waste matter. Nicotine in cigarette smoke makes the heart beat faster. This raises the pressure of the blood in your arteries, causing high blood pressure.

   a. What is the main idea of the paragraph? _____

   _____

   _____

   b. How does the circulatory system work? _____

   _____

   _____

   c. Why can cigarette smoking cause high blood pressure? _____

   _____

   _____

   _____

5. In many places, requests to limit smoking in public places are being made. For example, in both Arizona and Connecticut, smoking in public meetings is against the law. The New York City Council banned smoking in certain public places, such as classrooms, supermarkets, and elevators. Right now the fine is fifteen days in jail and a $50.00 fine. But once the law is better known, the penalty will be one year in jail and a $1,000 fine. Because of the difficulty in enforcing the law, the rules are always being broken.

   a. What is the main idea of the paragraph? _____

   _____

   _____

   b. Do the laws mentioned in the paragraph seem fair to you?

   _____ Why? _____

_____

_____

c. Do you think smoking should be illegal in public places? _____

Why? _____

_____

_____

B. Comprehending Short Essays: "Big Business: Selling Cancer"

Directions. Before you read the following essay, read the title and ask yourself what you think it is about. As you read the essay, ask yourself questions about what you are reading. Become involved in the subject of the essay.

BIG BUSINESS: SELLING CANCER

[1] Since the 1950s, more and more information has been publicized to show cigarette smoking is a health hazard. There is evidence that links smoking with cancer, heart problems, and lung disease (emphysema). Nevertheless, tobacco companies are making more profit than ever before. It seems the more dangerous smoking becomes, the more people smoke. Why? Cigarette advertising.

[2] When cigarette companies realized they could not fight the truth about the danger of smoking, they created the so-called low tar and nicotine cigarettes. Advertising was so well done that smokers went for these "new" cigarettes. Cigarette makers were able to almost double the number of cigarettes they could produce from the same amount of tobacco. Tobacco profits are so high now that tobacco companies are forced to find ways to spend their money. Many tobacco companies are buying up farm lands, cosmetic companies, canned food businesses, soap companies, and other industries not related to smoking. Rather than losing money, the cigarette industry has become more solid than ever. All this because advertising has convinced 50,000,000 people they should smoke.

[3] The smoker, the one who has made tobacco a big industry, is not doing as well. Many more smokers are developing cancer of the mouth,

lungs, or throat. Others have fallen victim to lung disease where they often live like vegetables for years. Still others are dying from circulatory disease. A well-known physician has said, "Cancer is probably the most merciful of the diseases related to smoking. It kills—usually in six months or less. . . . Emphysema is different. Any smoker simply has to smoke a large enough quantity over a long enough time and he will develop emphysema. Emphysema patients sometimes struggle on pathetically for five to ten years as vegetables—needing constant care 24 hours a day." In 1972, 300,000 people died as a result of smoking. This is more than the American losses in both the Korean and Vietnam wars.

[4] The U.S. Government's connection with the tobacco industry is interesting. They have been very careful to walk a middle line. They have forced the tobacco companies to put warning labels on their advertising and cigarette packs. But that's about it. They have to be cautious. Many Southern states' income depends on tobacco crops. Tax on tobacco at both the state and federal level is staggeringly high. And tobacco companies are big contributors to political campaigns. They spend millions on advertising, which helps the economy.

[5] In 1970, the U.S. Congress spent $84 million to help the tobacco industry. The government guarantees a minimum price per acre for tobacco crops. It spent $2.7 million in research to find a new way to grow tobacco more cheaply. It also spent $250,000 in advertising overseas to get foreign nations to buy American tobacco. In fact, the U.S. is the world's biggest tobacco exporter. And big business is more important than good health to some people.

[6] Even though cigarettes cannot be advertised on television, cigarette sales are higher than ever. Magazines, newspapers, billboards—all carry ads making cigarette smoking seem a pleasure. Advertisers make smoking seem fun, exciting, adult, and glamorous. We're even told they taste good:

"Tastefully Cool"—(Kool)
"The Great *New* Taste"—(Kent)
"Tastes as Fresh as Springtime"—(Salem)
"Taste One! Taste Me!"—(Doral)
"The Natural Choice for a Lady with Taste"—(Eve)
"It's a Matter of Taste"—(Viceroy)

Research shows that very few people can tell the difference between brands.

[7] Look carefully at any cigarette ad. Is it really selling cigarettes? More than likely it's selling an image, an idea that smoking is natural. The ads imply that smoking can win you a man or a woman. They imply you'll look like that rugged man or beautiful woman in the ad if you pop a cigarette in your mouth. They imply cigarettes are "fresh" and con-

"Give me a light; I can't stand the Springtime-fresh air!"

nected with green fields, running streams, or snow-covered mountains. The truth? Cigarettes kill.

[8] Cigarette companies even use the evidence against them to sell us. When lists are published showing which cigarettes are high or low in tar and nicotine, some companies claim, "Look at us; we don't kill you as fast as Brand X." And the idea that filters cut down the amount of tar and nicotine is a fantasy. Advertising, however, has convinced us smoking is safer now.

[9] One tobacco company recently claimed their cigarette was "a thinking man's cigarette." The truth is that if a man or woman were thinking for himself or herself, the tobacco industry would be out of business by now.

Comprehension Check

Directions. Discuss these questions in class. Your instructor may want you to write answers to some of them.

1. Does the title fit the main idea of the essay? Why?
2. What do you think about the government's connection with the tobacco industry?
3. Why are tobacco companies going into other businesses?
4. Who is responsible for the tobacco industry's success?
5. Why do you think more and more people are smoking even though it's a health hazard?
6. Explain the picture on page 228.
7. Do you think you are affected by advertising? Why?
8. Is the author of the essay biased? Is the essay a form of propaganda? Are you biased about smoking?

C. Comprehending This Chapter

Directions. As a review of this chapter, discuss or answer these questions.

1. What words at the beginning of the chapter (p. 203) do you need to review?
2. What are synonyms? Give some examples.
3. What are antonyms? Give some examples.
4. What is the importance of understanding word formation (changing words from nouns to verbs, and so on)?
5. What comprehension problems did you have in the last two drills?
6. Did you have trouble reading the last essay, "Big Business: Selling Cancer"? Explain.
7. What did you learn or relearn from working in this chapter?

CHAPTER 8

Objectives

P: PREREADING DRILLS

A. Words to Know
B. Warm-up Drills

R: READING DRILL

A. Reading and Thinking About What You Read
   "Shape Up, Bionic Woman!" by Ann Pincus
B. Comprehension Check

E: EXERCISES IN VOCABULARY

A. Drills
   1: Word Categories
   2: Greek Word Parts
   3: Latin Word Parts
   4: Root Words
   5: Words In Context
B. Vocabulary Check

P: PERFECTING READING SKILLS

A. Comprehending Paragraphs: Skimming and Scanning
B. Comprehending Essays: Skimming and Scanning
   "Making TV Commercials"
C. Comprehending This Chapter

OBJECTIVES

When you have finished with this chapter, you will

1. Recognize and be able to use 90 percent of the vocabulary words in the "Words to Know" section.

2. Know what is meant by "word categories."

3. Know the advantage of knowing word parts, such as roots, prefixes, and suffixes.

4. Know and be able to use at least eight Greek and Latin word parts.

5. Be able to name and know the meanings of at least ten words that contain Greek or Latin parts.

6. Be able to define skimming and scanning and to know when to use those skills.

7. Have developed your reading comprehension skills in locating the thesis or main idea of an essay, locating facts quickly through scanning, and general speed of reading comprehension.

P: PREREADING DRILLS

A. Words to Know

Directions. Read the following list of words aloud. Learn any you don't know. They all appear in the essay you will read in this chapter.

1. *bionic*—having to do with things made from a blend of the science of biology and electronics (bio–*bio*logy/nics–electro*nics*).

   The bionic woman on TV is fictional, but scientists are making bionic parts for those without arms or legs.

2. *imitating*—copying, doing as someone else does.

   The trouble with most TV programs is that they are not imitating real life or real people.

3. *protagonist*—the leading or main person in a story, the main character, the hero or heroine.

   Angie Dickinson was the female protagonist in the TV series "Police Woman."

4. *full-fledged*—matured, advanced, complete.

   After years of working as an assistant, she was finally promoted as a full-fledged producer.

5. *function*—job, task, work, duty (n.); to do or act as expected (v.).

   Mary's real function in the program is to give advice.

6. *colleagues*—fellow workers, partners, co-workers.

   Shelley says that her colleagues feel the same way she does.

7. *demoralize*—to upset, disturb, confuse, bother, weaken.

   If Harry fails that class, the experience will demoralize him.

8. *neurotic*—nervous, full of fear or anxiety.

   Rhoda is too neurotic to keep a job for long.

9. *botches*—messes up, fouls up, screws up.

   Her husband always botches up their bank account.

10. *offensively aggressive*—coming on so strong that it upsets people, too pushy.

Ann has few friends because she is offensively aggressive.

11. *tote*—to carry, haul.

    Angie is a cop and totes a gun.

12. *offshoot*—spin-off, outgrowth, result, outcome.

    The TV program "Rhoda" was an offshoot of "The Mary Tyler Moore Show."

13. *bigot*—a biased person who is narrow-minded.

    Archie Bunker from "All in the Family" is a bigot.

14. *klutz*—a clumsy or slow-witted person, a meathead.

    Archie thinks his son-in-law is a klutz.

15. *sitcom*—abbreviation for situation comedy, such as "Laverne and Shirley," "Rhoda," and "Soap."

    Television sitcoms are high in the ratings now.

16. *savoir faire*—manners, know-how, grace, experience.

    It's usually the men on TV programs who show wit, wisdom, and savoir faire.

17. *mentor*—a wise and trusted teacher or person.

    Kate can't seem to make a move without asking her mentor, her father.

18. *intrepid*—brave, fearless.

    Eve is an intrepid reporter who tracks down injustice wherever she finds it.

19. *miscarriage of justice*—bad management, poor handling of a trial case.

    If the judge lets the rapist go, it will be a miscarriage of justice.

20. *Burbank*—a city in California known as the television center.

    NBC's main television studios are in Burbank.

B. Warm-up Drills

Drill 1

Directions. Using the words or phrases from the "Words to Know" section above, write the correct words in the blanks in the following sentences.

1. Dee always _____ any job that requires thinking.

2. The _____ in the story is a young woman, twenty-five, single, and Chicana.

3. If the program is a success, there will probably be an _____ using one of the other characters.

4. Wonder Woman is an _____ heroine who seems afraid of nothing.

5. Let me _____ that bag for awhile.

6. If we are going to write a television script, we need the _____ of an experienced author.

7. Johnny is a real _____; he's always tripping over his feet.

8. Just a look at her bitten down fingernails shows how _____ Jan is.

9. My _____ and I are having a big office party Friday.

10. If the jury finds the Fonz guilty, it will be a gross _____.

11. Television is boring because when one network has a success, the others try _____ it.

12. If you don't quit telling me how badly I did, you will

_____ me to the point where I'll just give up.

13. Those _____ on the jury are so narrow-

minded that it scares me.

14. Scientists are perfecting _____ arms and

legs, but they won't have the power the television characters do.

15. Now that I have my license, I'm a _____

beautician.

---

1. botches, 2. protagonist, 3. offshoot, 4. intrepid, 5. tote,
6. savoir faire, 7. klutz, 8. neurotic, 9. colleagues, 10. miscarriage of
justice, 11. imitating, 12. demoralize, 13. bigots, 14. bionic,
15. full-fledged.

Drill 2

Directions. Move your eyes from left to right. Mark the word by the number every time it appears on the same line. Work rapidly. Don't look back on a line. Don't change any errors. Try to finish in thirty-five seconds or less.
Begin timing.

1. heroes   heroine   hero   heroine   heroes   heroes
2. switch   switch   swatch   swarm   switch   swam
3. imitate   imitating   imitated   imitate   imitation   imitate
4. worth   worthy   worth   would   worthless   worth
5. draw   drew   draw   drawn   drew   draw
6. female   female   male   femor   female   friend
7. women   woman   woman   women   woman   women
8. examine   exams   examine   examined   exam   examine
9. producer   produce   produced   produce   producer   product
10. promote   promise   promote   promise   promote   problem
11. studio   studio   study   started   studs   studio
12. feminist   female   feminist   female   female   feminist
13. function   luncheon   functional   function   funky   function
14. routine   route   routine   routine   route   routes
15. manager   marriages   manager   manages   manager   manages

TIME: _____

Check each line carefully. Make sure you marked the correct word each time it appears. Learn any words you don't know.

TOTAL LINES CORRECT: _____

Drill 3

Directions. Follow the same directions as for the last drill. Try to finish in thirty seconds or less.
Begin timing.

1. should	shoulder shoulder **should** **should** shoulder
2. botches	butcher **botches** butcher butcher **botches**
3. accounts	accent counts **accounts** counts accents
4. villains	village **villains** village vile **villains**
5. offense	offensive **offense** offers offend **offense**
6. aggressive	agreement oppressive **aggressive** agreement
7. apparently	**apparently** apparent parent appears **apparently**
8. envy	every even ever **envy** envious **envy**
9. flirt	**flirt** flit flies **flirt** flopped flip
10. motivation	motive motivate **motivation** motives **motivation**
11. portray	portal **portray** portrait **portray** portal
12. involved	invite involvement involve **involved** involves
13. inspired	inspite **inspired** inspire inspite **inspired**
14. daring	darling **daring** darling **daring** darling
15. cameras	cameo **cameras** camera camera **cameras**

TIME: _____

Check each line carefully. Make sure you marked the correct word everytime it appears. Learn any words you don't know.

TOTAL LINES CORRECT: _____

Drill 4

Directions. Follow the same directions as for the last drill. The only difference here is that you will be looking for a short phrase, not a single word. Try to finish in forty seconds or less.
Begin timing.

1. a couple of   a lot of   a few of   a couple of
a couple is

2. make-believe heroes   make-believe hams   make-believe heroes
make-believe show

3. larger-then-life   smaller-than-life   larger-than-life
larger-than-life

4. more recently   more receivers   more recent
more recently

5. not at all   not at me   not at home   not at all

6. private life   prior life   private life   private talks

7. for that matter   for that mother   for that matter
for that middle

8. a role model   a role model   a role maker   a role model

9. on the ball   on the bench   on the road   on the ball

10. a little wart   a little wad   a little wart   a little while

11. playing up to   praying up to   playing up to
playing up to

12. track down   track down   trick down   track down

13. makes a pass   make a pan   makes a puss
makes a push

14. create someone   create some   create some
create someone

15. on the verge   on the vine   on the verge   on the hedge

Time: _____

Check each line carefully. Make sure you marked the correct phrase. Sometimes it appears more than once on a line. Notice there is no phrase for line 13. Did you go back and look again? Remember, don't look back on a line. It slows you down.

Total lines correct: _____

Drill 5

Directions. Follow the same directions as for the last drill. Try to finish in thirty-five seconds or less. Don't look back on a line.
Begin timing.

1. shape up	ship out sharp urge shape up
2. intrepid girl	intrepid girl interested guy intrepid girl
3. for that matter	for that mother for that much for that matter
4. offensively aggressive	offensively angry offensive aunt offensively aggressive
5. stays at home	stays at school stays at home stays lost
6. hopelessly dizzy	helplessly dopey hoplessly dumb hopelessly dizzy
7. go along with	go away with go along way go along with
8. schoolgirl idol	schoolgirl crush schoolgirl idol schoolboy charm
9. dramatic series	dramatic serial drama school dramatic scene
10. disappointed me	disappointed you disappointed her disappointed me
11. manages to be	manager to be manages to be manages me
12. had hysterics	had hysteria had hysterics had hyterics
13. much better	much better much butter much batter
14. difficult decisions	difficult day difficult decisions different decisions
15. fought injustice	fight injustice fought injury fought injustice

TIME: _____

Check each line carefully. Make sure you marked each phrase every time it appears on the same line. There is no phrase on line 9. Did you go back and try to find one, or did you move on as you were directed?

TOTAL LINES CORRECT: _____

Drill 6

Directions. The essay you will be reading in this chapter mentions several TV programs, actors, and characters in books. See if you can match the names in the left-hand column with the names in the right-hand column. Some can be used more than once. This is just a "trivia" test for the fun of it.

_____ 1. The Fonz		a. "Star Trek"
_____ 2. Mary Richards		b. "All's Fair"
_____ 3. Mr. Spock		c. "Police Woman"
_____ 4. Steve Austin		d. "Happy Days"
_____ 5. Charley		e. "Wonder Woman"
_____ 6. Angie Dickinson		f. "Six Million Dollar Man"
_____ 7. Major Trevor		g. "Mary Tyler Moore Show"
_____ 8. Becky Thatcher		h. *Tom Sawyer*
_____ 9. Lieutenant Uhura		i. "The Avengers"
_____ 10. Mrs. Steed		

Check your answers with these:
1. d, 2. g, 3. a, 4. f, 5. b, 6. c, 7. e, 8. h, 9. a, 10. i.

R: READING DRILL

A. Reading and Thinking About What You Read

Directions. Answer the following questions.

1. Read the title of the essay below. What can you guess will be the
subject of the essay? _____

_____

_____

2. Read the opening paragraph. What now can you tell about the main
idea of the essay? _____

_____

_____

3. Read the last three short paragraphs. What do those paragraphs tell
you about the main idea of the essay? _____

_____

_____

_____

4. Why is it sometimes a good idea to look at the title, opening, and clos-
ing paragraphs of an essay? _____

_____

_____

Now read the essay. Look for the main idea and how the author sup-
ports her thesis. (A thesis is what point the author is trying to make

about the subject of the essay.) The essay may seem dated because the "Bionic Woman" is no longer being made. But think about new television programs dealing with women. Has there been much of a change in the way women are portrayed on TV since this article was written? Is the author still correct in her opinions?

SHAPE UP, BIONIC WOMAN!
Ann Pincus

[1] My daughter Battle is 6 years old. Her brothers, Adam and Ward, are 8½ and 10 years old, respectively. They watch a lot of TV programs. The boys even draw their make-believe heroes from the tube. A couple of years ago, their idols were Batman and Robin; last year they switched to Captain Kirk and Mr. Spock. More recently, they've been imitating "The Fonz" and Kotter. They identify closely with these larger-than-life heroes.

[2] Who is there for my daughter to identify with? Lieutenant Uhura? Laverne and Shirley?

[3] My answer is: THERE IS NO ONE. There is not one larger-than-life heroine worth mentioning, or one female life-style worth imitating. There aren't any at 7 o'clock at night and there wouldn't be any if I let her stay up seven nights a week until the 11 o'clock news.

[4] Someone may say, "Oh, that's not at all true any more!" There's Wonder Woman and the Bionic Woman, even Police Woman. There's Mary Tyler Moore and Rhoda and Maude and Phyllis. This fall there's even Charley, the female protagonist in Norman Lear's new sitcom, "Alls' Fair."

[5] True, these are shows about women. But are these women drawn from life? Are any of them heroines? Would anybody want to be like any of them? For that matter, *should* anybody want to be like any of them? Let's examine the kind of images they project.

[6] Mary Tyler Moore . . . started out six years ago as an assistant producer in name, but a girl Friday in fact, at a Minneapolis television studio. A couple of years ago, she got promoted to a full-fledged producer (a crumb dropped to the feminist movement), but her real function in the program—to play Ann Landers to her TV colleagues—has not changed.

[7] The private life of TV's Mary Richards would demoralize the real Ann Landers. Despite the fact that she's had at least a dozen boyfriends over the years, she still has trouble telling a man what she thinks about

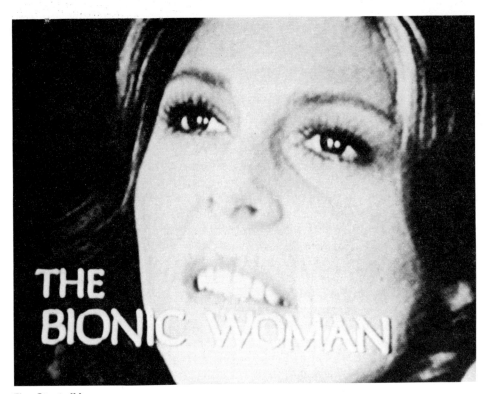

The Bionic Woman

him. She must be close to 40 in TV age, yet when a man makes a pass at her, she manages to put on the "oh, gee whiz, golly, what'll I do" routine.

[8] It may be great entertainment but she's not a great role model.

[9] Rhoda has trouble with her job (and her husband) because she's so neurotic. Phyllis can't keep a job (or a man) because she's too dumb. Maude, who clearly is more intelligent and has more on the ball than her husband—a little wart named Walter—stays at home while her husband botches up their bank accounts at the office. Maude also suffers from being on the verge of hysteria all the time. Perhaps that's the reason she doesn't get a job.

[10] Mary Hartman doesn't count, but Charley of "All's Fair" does because she has a real-life job. She is a photographer for a newsweekly, yet she is hopelessly dizzy, offensively aggressive and stupid. She couldn't get a job selling Instamatic cameras, much less using a Leica.

[11] What kind of role model is that?

[12] Angie Dickinson as Police Woman certainly landed a good job with the LAPD. It apparently pays well because she wears clothes that would make Jackie O green with envy. I may be wrong, but it seems to

me she got her job by playing up to the boss. She certainly is a flirt. She does tote a gun and go along with the boys to track down the bad guys, but she tends to get caught by the villains—due to mistakes such as tripping over a twig or some other clever move—and has to be rescued by her colleagues.

[13] Wonder Woman has possibilities. But her only motivation to right wrongs appears to be to save her beloved Major Trevor from harm. That leaves only the Bionic Woman, the Eve-like offshoot of the Six Million Dollar Man who miraculously manages to be weaker than he even though they have the same machines in their mechanical legs.

[14] Now, you will say (alas, my husband has already said it) that the male-role models seen on television are not positive either, that some men are portrayed as bigots and most act like klutzes. But you are wrong. And my husband is wrong. Men in television, whether in sitcoms or dramatic series, ordinarily are the Decision Makers, the Problem Solvers. It is their wit or wisdom or *savoir faire* that tricks the villain. Just look at Columbo or Kojak or Starsky and Hutch or Steve Austin, the guys in "Switch" or "M*A*S*H" or "Hawaii Five-O," or Raymond Burr in any of his incarnations.

[15] There have, of course, been women on TV who dealt with "life." Good or bad, they quickly disappeared. Remember Faye, the gay divorcee? Kate McShane was another *involved* woman. She was a lawyer, and by inference a good role model. Unfortunately she couldn't make a move without consulting her brother, the priest, or her father, the mentor. "McNaughton's Daughter" was much better. She, too, was a lawyer who fought injustice, and she managed to be self-sufficient. She didn't even last one season.

[16] It must be said that true heroines are hard to find in any kind of fiction. Tom Sawyer was brave and daring while Becky Thatcher had hysterics in the cave. And my favorite schoolgirl idol, Jo March of "Little Women," finally disappointed me. It was fine and noble to run a school for the needy. But why did it have to be a school mainly for boys? What about the girls?

[17] There was at least one role model for young girls to identify with on the radio 25 or 30 years ago. Her name was Lorelei Kilbourne and no doubt she inspired a whole generation of women to become journalists. She was the intrepid girl reporter who, with Steve Wilson, tracked down many a miscarriage of justice on "Big Town." She was wonderful. She had a real job. She was paid for her work. She was good at it. She made difficult decisions and, as far as I know, she didn't quit to get married.

[18] Why can't television create someone like that? A more accurate question is: why can't *American* television create someone like that? British television created just such a character in "The Avengers" about fifteen years ago.

[19] At least television programs should have women in them who are

wives, mothers and working women. More and more American women juggle all three jobs; why shouldn't the television screen reflect that?

[20] We've had the Bionic Woman. Now let's try for a Three-Dimensional Woman.

[21] Burbank, can you hear me?

Mary and Rhoda (Photograph: Culver Pictures, Inc.)

B. Comprehension Check

Directions. Answer the following questions without looking back.

Recall

1. Circle the letter of the statement below that best says what the thesis, or main idea of the essay, is.
   a. Television does not have heroes for boys to model themselves after.
   b. Television does not have heroines for girls to model themselves after.
   c. Television programs should have more women in them who are wives, mothers, and working women.
   d. Radio had better women role models than television does.
2. T or F. The author thinks Mary Tyler Moore is a good role model for young girls.
3. T or F. The author feels the male role models on TV are better than the women's because the men, at least, are decision makers and problem solvers.
4. T or F. The author feels that there have never been women on TV who have dealt with "life."

Interpretation

5. What does the title mean? How is it connected to the thesis? _____

_____

_____

6. Would you say that the author watches a lot of television? _____

Why? _____

_____

_____

7. What does the author mean when she says television should try for a

"Three-Dimensional Woman"? _____

_____

_____

8. The author says that Charley of "All's Fair" (no longer on TV) "couldn't get a job selling Instamatic cameras, much less using a Leica," an expensive camera. Why is this contrast a "put-down" of Charley? _____

_____

_____

Application

9. Do you think television programs should have characters that young people can model themselves after? _____ Why? _____

_____

_____

10. Do you think the author is right about the way women are portrayed on TV? _____

_____

_____

E: EXERCISES IN VOCABULARY

A. Drills

Drill 1: Word Categories (Part A)

Directions. Below are some general words. In the blank beside the specific words, write in the general word that belongs. The first one is done for you. Some words can be used more than once.

fruit   television   city   animal
person   automobile   state   sport

1. Burbank *city*

2. tennis _____

3. Sylvania _____

4. horse _____

5. Iowa _____

6. orange _____

7. Joe _____

8. Toyota _____

9. football _____

10. elephant _____

11. peach _____

12. convertible _____

Drill 1: Word Categories (Part B)

Directions. Some words imply or suggest something more than their dictionary meaning. For example, a *siren* suggests *trouble;* a *badge* suggests *authority* or *power*. In the blanks below, write in a word from the right-hand column that shows what the word by the number suggests or implies. The drill is continued on the next page.

1. hospital _____

2. rattlesnake _____

3. handshake _____

4. scrapbook _____

5. laughter _____

a. friendly

b. happiness

c. learning

d. illness

e. recognition

6. school _____   f. danger

7. diamonds _____   g. affection

8. award _____   h. unlucky

9. kiss _____   i. wealth

10. thirteen _____   j. memories

Check your answers with these:
Part A: 2. sport, 3. television, 4. animal, 5. state, 6. fruit, 7. person, 8. automobile, 9. sport, 10. animal, 11. fruit, 12. automobile. *Part B:* 1. illness, 2. danger, 3. friendly, 4. memories, 5. happiness, 6. learning, 7. wealth, 8. recognition, 9. affection, 10. unlucky.

Drill 2: Greek Word Parts (Part A)

Directions. Many English words come from Greek prefixes and roots. Study the Greek word parts below. Then answer the questions that follow.

anti = against	*phone* = sound
graph, gram = writing, record	*scope* = sight
micro = small	*tele* = far

1. Explain why a *telephone* is called what it is. _____

   _____

   _____

2. Why is a *microscope* called what it is? _____

   _____

   _____

3. How does a *microscope* differ from a *telescope?* _____

   _____

   _____

4. How does a *telephone* differ from a *telegram?* _____

_____

_____

5. If a person is against having or using telephones, what one word

could you make up that would mean this? _____

_____

Drill 2: Greek Word Parts (Part B)

Directions. Study the Greek word parts below. Then answer the questions that follow. You may need to refer to Part A for some answers. Also, when two word parts are joined and the first part ends with a vowel and the second part begins with a vowel, the vowel in the second part is dropped *(geoølogy, bioølogy).*

auto = self
bio = life
geo = earth

hydro = water
meter = measure
ology = study of

1. If *auto* means self and *graph* means writing, what is an autograph?

_____

2. If *bio* means life and *ology* means study of, what is *biology?*

_____

3. If *hydro* means water and *meter* means measure, what is a *hydro-meter?*

_____

4. What word means the study of the earth?

_____

5. What word means the study of water?

_____

6. What word means a life story or record of someone?

_____

7. What word means a life story written by the person it's about?

_____

8. What word means an instrument that measures small things?

_____

9. What word means an instrument that picks up sounds in the water?

_____

10. Why is a phonograph called what it is?

_____

Check your answers with these. Your wording may be different.
Part A
1. It brings us sounds (voices) from a distance, or far away.
2. We see small things better with it, such as germs.
3. The first helps us see small things better; the second brings things from a distance so that we can see them better.
4. The first brings us sound from afar; the second is a written message from afar.
5. antitelephone.
Part B
1. Actually, someone's signature or name written by that person, 2. study of life, 3. an instrument that measures water, 4. geology, 5. hydrology, 6. biography, 7. autobiography, 8. micrometer, 9. hydroplane, 10. It's a record of sound.

Drill 3: Latin Word Parts

Directions. Many English words are also made up of Latin word parts. Study the Latin word parts below.

inter = between, among	*aqua* = water
mis = wrong, incorrect	*port* = carry
non = not	*spec*(t) = look
post = after	*via, vis* = see
trans = across	*voc* = call

Using the word parts above and the key words in the definitions below, make English words that fit the following definitions. The first one has been done for you. Notice how the Latin word part above was added to the key word *mingle* in this definition.

1. to mingle among people   *intermingle*

2. to carry across   _____

3. able to be seen   _____

4. not a resident   _____

5. after the conference   _____

6. a tank for fish   _____

7. spelled wrong   _____

8. talks a lot   _____

9. to look into something   _____

10. something you can carry   _____

11. someone who looks on   _____

12. across the Atlantic   _____

Check your answers with these.
1. intermingle, 2. transport, 3. visible, 4. nonresident, 5. postconference, 6. aquarium, 7. misspelled, 8. vocal, 9. inspect, 10. portable, 11. spectator, 12. transatlantic.

Drill 4: Root Words

Directions. Below are some phrase groups. In each group, three of the four phrases have words that are from the same root or root word. Check the blank in front of the phrase that does *not* have a word from the same root or root word. Write the root or root word in the blank space. For example:

    a. _____ a changeable person
    b. _____ the changing weather
    c. ✓ the chained bear
    d. _____ the unchanged man

    Root word: *change*

Notice that the root word is *change* except for the third phrase.

1. a. ____ the invisible man

   b. ____ visibility is high

   c. ____ poor vision

   d. ____ division of work

   Root: _____

2. a. ____ a portable TV

   b. ____ portray a villain

   c. ____ good transportation

   d. ____ import tax

   Root: _____

3. a. ____ the new inspector

   b. ____ spectator sports

   c. ____ new spectacles

   d. ____ strange spector

   Root: _____

4. a. ____ no plans now

   b. ____ a late plane

   c. ____ the planning stages

   d. ____ planned to go

   Root word: _____

5. a. ____ a creative mind

   b. ____ create your own

   c. ____ a lovely creation

   d. ____ strange creature

   Root word: _____

6. a. ____ it's unreal

   b. ____ realize now

   c. ____ face reality

   d. ____ into real estate

   Root word: _____

7. a. ____ equal opportunity

   b. ____ equipped wrong

   c. ____ unequal pay

   d. ____ equally measured

   Root word: _____

8. a. ____ probably true

   b. ____ improbable mess

   c. ____ preferable to this

   d. ____ not probable

   Root word: _____

Drill 5: Words in Context (Part A)

Directions. Below is a list of words. Write the correct word in the blanks
in the paragraph that follows.

fact   yet   demoralize
trouble   pass   boyfriends
manages   routine   role

The private life of TV's Mary Richards would (1) _____

_____ the real Ann Landers. Despite the (2) _____

_____ that she's had at least a dozen (3) _____

_____ over the years, she still has (4) _____

telling a man what she thinks of him. She must be close to 40 in TV age,

(5) _____ when a man makes a (6) _____

_____ at her, she (7) _____ to put on the

"Oh, gee whiz, golly, what'll I do" (8) _____. It

may be great entertainment but she's not a great (9) _____

_____ model.

Drill 5: Words in Context (Part B)

Directions. Using Part A, write your own words in the blanks. You can
be funny or serious. Read your answers in class.

B. Vocabulary Check

Part A

Directions. In the blanks, write in the letter of the word from the right-hand column that tells what the word by the number suggests or implies. The first one has been done for you.

_c_ 1. diamonds   a. unlucky

_____ 2. yellow   b. unhappy

_____ 3. thirteen   c. wealth

_____ 4. handshake   d. approval

_____ 5. laughter   e. happiness

_____ 6. danger   f. coward

_____ 7. crying   g. illness

_____ 8. hospital   h. authority

_____ 9. badge   i. red

_____ 10. applause   j. friendly

Part B

Directions. Define the following word parts.

1. tele: _____

2. micro: _____

3. phone: _____

4. graph: _____

5. ology: _____

6. auto: _____

7. geo: _____

8. meter: _____

9. bio: _____

10. scope: _____

Part C

Directions. Using the word parts from Part B, write five words and define each one.

1. word: _____

   definition: _____

2. word: _____

   definition: _____

3. word: _____

   definition: _____

4. word: _____

   definition: _____

5. word: _____

   definition: _____

Part D

Directions. Define the following words.

1. transport: _____

2. intermingle: _____

3. vocal: _____

4. inspect: _____

5. spectator: _____

6. nonresident: _____

7. invisible: ———————————————————————————————

8. postwar: ———————————————————————————————

9. portable: ———————————————————————————————

10. aquarium: ———————————————————————————————

NAME ——————————————————— SECTION ————————— DATE —————————

P: PERFECTING READING SKILLS

A. Comprehending Paragraphs: Skimming and Scanning

Directions. Skimming is quickly looking over something to get some general idea what it is about. Scanning is quickly looking over something to find a specific thing, such as a name, a date, a page number, or a word in a dictionary. Skim, don't read, the following paragraphs and answer the skimming and scanning questions. Try to take less than twenty seconds to skim each paragraph.

1. Just skim over the paragraph below. Don't read it.

The TV quiz show is really a form of advertising. The amount of advertising on TV is limited to the times available. To get around this, the TV quiz show was created. The quiz show allows dozens of products to be seen on TV outside the paid commercial time. Manufacturers give free products and sometimes pay a fee to have their name mentioned when someone wins their product. A study of TV quiz shows revealed that as much as 40 percent of a thirty-minute show was given over to some form of advertising.

Skimming Questions (Don't look back at the paragraph.)

a. What is the paragraph about? _____

_____

b. Why was the TV show created? _____

_____

Scanning Questions (Scan back over the paragraph for answers to these questions)

c. What percentage of a thirty-minute quiz show is given to some

form of advertising? _____

d. Do manufacturers pay a fee to have their name mentioned on quiz

shows? _____

2. In twenty seconds or less, skim over the paragraph below. Don't read it.

Automobile makers give free cars to TV series if their brand is made to look good. The "good guys" on the show will use the free cars provided. The "bad guys" will use a different brand. Mannix always used to drive a Chevrolet Camaro. Mod Squad members drove a Chrysler. Starsky and Hutch drive a Ford Torino. A Firebird is used on "The Rockford Files." Notice how "good" shots or scenes using the free car show up in programs of this type. A Chrysler official says that the cars they "donate" to the program must be used right. If they aren't, they point it out to the TV show's producer. The number of cars given is reduced if their product isn't given enough show time.

Skimming Questions (Don't look back)

a. What is the paragraph about? _____

_____

b. What brands of cars are mentioned? _____

_____

Scanning Questions (Scan back over the paragraph)

c. What happens if a "donated" brand car does not get the coverage

on TV that the manufacturers want? _____

_____

_____

d. Why do auto makers give free cars to some TV series? _____

_____

_____

3. In twenty seconds or less, skim the paragraph below. Don't read it.

The average American spends more time watching TV than any other activity but sleep. For millions, the time they go to bed depends on when the late news is over or whether or not Johnny Carson will be on the "Tonight Show." Even bathroom habits are controlled by TV. The water department in one city proved this. When the movie *Airport* was shown on TV, there was a record drop on the water department gauges at 9:00 P.M. Why? It seems that at 8:30 P.M., a bomb exploded on the airplane in the movie. Little water was used during this time. But when the pilot landed the plane safely and the movie ended, 26,000 people flushed their toilets causing 80,000 gallons of water to be used at the same time. The power of television seems to be controlling even our toilet habits.

Skimming Questions (Don't look back)

a. What is the main idea of the paragraph? _____

_____

b. What example is used to back up the main idea of the paragraph?

_____

_____

Scanning Questions (Scan back for answers)

c. When did the water gauges drop? _____ _____

_____

d. How many people flushed their toilets at the same time? _____

_____

4. In twenty seconds or less, skim the paragraph below. Don't read it.

Children aged five and under, watch an average of 23.5 hours of TV a week. (Adults watch 44 hours per week.) This means that by the time the child graduates from high school, he or she will have watched about 15,000 hours of TV. He or she will have seen 350,000 commercials and watched 18,000 murders. Next to parents, TV has become the most powerful influence on the beliefs, attitudes, and values of young people. Television is affecting the way humans learn to become human beings. Based on what is on TV, the human race is in trouble.

Skimming Questions (Don't look back):

a. What is the main idea of the paragraph? _____

_____

_____

b. Does the author approve of young people watching so much TV?

_____

Scanning Questions (Scan for the answers):

c. How many hours of TV per week does the average adult watch?

_____

d. How many commercials has the average high school graduate

watched? _____

e. Next to parents, TV has become the most powerful influence on the

_____, _____, and _____

_____ of young people.

Discuss your answers in class. Also discuss how you skimmed and scanned the paragraphs.

The information in the above paragraphs has been taken from Jeffrey Schrank's *Snap, Crackle, and Popular Taste*, Dell, 1977.

B. Comprehending Essays: Skimming and Scanning

Directions. Don't read the following essay. Skim over it. Take less than a minute to do this. Then answer the questions that follow the essay.

MAKING TV COMMERCIALS

[1] According to the magazine *Advertising Age*, last year $26.7 billion was spent on advertising. Television advertising alone cost $4.85 billion. For most of us billions of dollars are too much to really comprehend. Let's put it this way. If you want to sell something on television, it will cost you almost $60,000 for just 30 seconds of prime time on a top-rated show.

[2] Now those large dollar numbers represent only the cost of *time*.

The cost of writing, designing, and filming an ad for TV can be more than $200,000 for one 30-second commercial. Polaroid Camera paid Laurence Olivier $250,000 to do an ad for them. It's reported that John Wayne received over a million dollars to do a series of commercials for Great Western Savings!

[3] Making an advertisement for television often costs more to make than a movie. Take a two-hour movie that costs $6 million to make. Costs average out to about $50,000 a minute, or $833 a second. A TV commercial can cost more than $6,000 a second. And that does not include the cost of paying for air time.

[4] A television network, such as CBS, NBC, or ABC, pays about $300,000 for a one-hour show of a TV series. That's about $5,000 a minute, or $85 a second. Compare $85 a second with $6,000 a second for a TV commercial. Which one is more valuable, the program or the ad? In terms of money—and making money is what television is all about—the commercial is by far more important.

[5] Because of the importance of a TV ad, advertising agencies do much preparation before shooting a commercial. Research, market testing, talent, time and money—all come together to make us want to buy a product. No matter how bad we think a commercial is, it works. Jeff Greenfield wrote in his article "Down to the Last Detail," that ". . . Charmin bathroom tissue commercials (they can't bear to call it toilet paper) will be a contributing factor to the fall of American civilization, should that happen. But those commercials carved out a substantial share of the market for a product that had nothing unusual to offer except a public impression formed from advertising."

[6] In other words, we may think it's silly to hear the store owner say, "Please don't squeeze the Charmin." But silly or not, the commercial works. The sales of Charmin went up once the ads began. TV commercials actually buy their way into our heads. We, in turn, buy the product.

[7] And the ads work because so much time and attention are given them. For example, making a beer ad is not easy. An advertising man tells of the effort that went into making one 30-second commercial. "The 'pour' shot is the key to a beer ad. How the beer looks going down the glass; whether the glass is completely clean and suggests ice-cold beer; how the bubbles look, whether the head on the beer is big enough, but not too big. Our standard order for a 'pour' shot was ten cases of beer—240 cans. And it wasn't overdoing it. I remember one pour shot which took 124 takes before the beer looked exactly right."

[8] Such attention and time goes into making all ads. Here are some rules of commercial ad making. If you want to get the blue-collar, lower-middle-class buyer, make sure the announcer has a tough, manly voice. Put some people in the ad who look like they work with their hands. If you want to sell to an upper-class audience, make sure that the house, the furniture, the books on the shelves, the clothes, the hair style, and so forth are the type that group identifies with. If you want to make the

buyer feel superior to the character selling the product, then make that person so stupid or silly everyone will feel great about himself or herself.

[9] We laugh at commercials. We think we're above them. We think they don't affect us. We don't think we pay that much attention to them. But evidence shows we are kidding ourselves. The making of a TV commercial that costs more than $6,000 a second, plus the cost of buying TV time is not kid stuff. It's big, big business. And it's telling us what to think, what we need, and what to buy. To put it simply, the TV commercial is a legal form of brainwashing.

Skimming Questions
See if you can answer these questions without looking back at the article.

1. What is the thesis, or main idea of the essay? _____

   _____

   _____

2. Which costs more, making a television commercial or a two-hour

   movie? _____

3. List at least four things you remember from skimming the essay.

   _____

   _____

   _____

   _____

Scanning Questions
Scan back through the essay to answer these questions.

4. How much money was spent on TV advertising last year? _____

   _____

5. What does it cost per second to make a two-hour movie? _____

   _____

6. What does it cost per second to make a 30-second commercial? _____

_____

7. How many cans of beer are usually ordered to make a "pour" ad?

_____

8. What is the point of paragraph 4? _____

_____

9. What is the point of paragraph 9? _____

_____

Discuss your answers in class.

C. Comprehending This Chapter

Directions. Answer the following questions as a review of this chapter. Your instructor may ask you to write on one or more questions.

1. What words from the beginning of this chapter (p. 232) do you need to review?
2. What is meant by "word categories"?
3. Name at least eight Greek or Latin word parts.
4. Name at least ten words that contain Greek or Latin word parts.
5. What advantage is there in knowing word parts, such as roots, prefixes, and suffixes?
6. Define skimming and scanning. When are these reading skills helpful?
7. What comprehension problems did you have, if any, in this chapter.
8. What did you learn or relearn from working in this chapter?
9. Did you enjoy doing any of the drills in this chapter? Why?

CHAPTER 9

Objectives

P: PREREADING DRILLS

A. Words to Know
B. Warm-up Drills

R: READING DRILL

A. Reading and Thinking About What You Read
   "UFOs. Real or Unreal?" by Robert Kraske
B. Comprehension Check

E: EXERCISES IN VOCABULARY

A. Drills
   1: Word Categories
   2: Greek Word Parts
   3: Latin Word Parts
   4: Root Words
   5: Words in Context
B. Vocabulary Check

P: PERFECTING READING SKILLS

A. Comprehending Reference Materials
B. Comprehending Maps, Tables, and Graphs
C. Comprehending This Chapter

OBJECTIVES

When you have finished this chapter, you will

1. Recognize and be able to use at least 90 percent of the vocabulary words from the "Words to Know" section.

2. Have developed your ability to organize information by dealing with word categories.

3. Have developed your ability to make and understand outlines.

4. Know and be able to use at least fifteen more Greek and Latin word parts.

5. Be able to name and use at least twenty more words containing Greek and Latin word parts.

6. Have developed further your ability to deal with words in context.

7. Have developed your ability to use skimming and scanning skills with reference materials such as a table of contents, an index, a glossary, maps, tables, and graphs.

8. Have developed your reading skills in all areas of comprehension.

P: PREREADING DRILLS

A. Words to Know

Directions. Read the following words aloud. Learn the definitions of any words you don't know.

1. *peer*—to look long at something, to stare.

   José peered at the strange object in the sky.

2. *coined*—invented a word or phrase.

   The term "flying saucer" was coined by a reporter.

3. *cirrus clouds*—high clouds made up of narrow, thin bands.

   The cirrus clouds made it difficult to spot UFOs.

4. *mirage*—an illusion, something not real, a hallucination.

   Did José really see a flying saucer, or was it a mirage?

5. *hallucination*—a delusion, something unreal, a mirage.

   The Air Force seems to think most UFO sightings are hallucinations.

6. *hoax*—a trick, a deception.

   Some UFO reports are not hallucinations, but hoaxes.

7. *haughtily*—overly proud, feeling superior to others, stuck-up.

   Teri drew herself up haughtily and said, "I did too see a UFO!"

8. *discredit*—to prove false, to expose, to disprove.

   Hoaxes and hallucinations tend to discredit UFO sightings.

9. *extensive*—far-reaching, wide-ranging, broad, big.

   There have been extensive investigations of UFO reports.

10. *justified*—excused, allowed or permitted for good reason.

    Some politicians feel that extensive study of UFOs can't be justified to the taxpayer.

11. *expectation*—the act of looking forward to something, hope.

    Some scientists have no great expectations that the study of UFOs will advance science's understanding of space.

12. *parallel*—side by side.

The UFO flew parallel with the space capsule for about ten minutes.

13. *temperature inversion*—when the air temperature increases with altitude, holding surface air down along with air pollution.

Because of temperature inversion, air pollution was high today.

14. *luminous*—bright, clear, shiny, brilliant.

Four pilots saw the luminous objects speed into space.

15. *indentation*—a deep notch or dent.

When they examined the area where the UFO landed, they found four indentations in the ground.

16. *charred*—burned, scorched.

A charred body was found in the wreck.

17. *debris*—remains of something broken or destroyed.

Russia and the United States have left satellites and other space debris in orbit.

18. *surveillance*—close watch, observation, lookout.

Some people believe that UFOs are surveillance devices of a more advanced technology than that known on earth.

19. *extraterrestial*—outside the earth's atmosphere.

Are UFOs really manned by extraterrestial beings keeping a surveillance on earth's actions?

20. *galaxy*—any of many large groups of stars, like the Milky Way.

Some day man may travel from galaxy to galaxy, which will be called intergalactic travel.

B. Warm-up Drills

Drill 1

Directions. Read the following sentences. Using the words from Part A, write in the correct word in each blank.

1. Keep a close _____ on the skyline.

2. We may soon be visited by _____ beings from another galaxy.

3. If you just made up that term, you just _____ a new phrase.

4. The Air Force claims that the UFO Tom says he saw was a _____ _____.

5. Scientists are trying to _____ Tom's story.

6. Tom feels _____ in trying to prove his story.

7. The details Tom gave of his UFO sighting were _____ _____ and impressive.

8. He has little _____ that they will believe him.

9. Too many people believe Tom is playing a _____ _____ on everyone.

10. Manuel likes to _____ through the binoculars.

Check your answers with these:
1. surveillance, 2. extraterrestial, 3. coined, 4. mirage *or* hallucination,
5. discredit, 6. justified, 7. extensive, 8. expectation, 9. hoax, 10. peer.

Drill 2

Directions. Read from left to right. Mark the word by the number each time it appears on the same line. Don't look back on the same line. Don't change any errors you may make. Work rapidly. Try to finish in thirty-five seconds or less.

Begin timing.

1. weather   whether   weather   whether   weather   whether
2. further   further   farther   farther   farther   further
3. former   farmer   former   former   farmer   farmer
4. tended   tender   tender   tended   tender   tender
5. sightings   sighings   sightings   sighings   signings   signtings
6. ridge   ridge   bridge   ridge   bridge   ridge
7. radar   radio   radar   redder   radar   radio
8. gulley   galley   galley   gulley   galley   gulley
9. orbit   order   orbit   order   orbit   order
10. booster   brother   bother   booster   brother   booster
11. tumble   tumbling   thumb   thimble   tumbled   thumb
12. debris   debris   debts   debris   debts   depth
13. advance   advice   advances   advancement   advance   advance
14. mirage   mirror   mirage   mirage   mirror   minor
15. hoaxes   horses   horses   hoaxes   horses   hoaxes

TIME: _____

Check each line to see if you marked the correct word. Learn the meanings of any words you don't know. Notice there is no word to mark on for item 11. Did you look back on that line?

TOTAL LINES CORRECT: _____

Drill 3

Directions. Follow the same directions as for the previous drill. Try to finish in thirty-five seconds or less.
Begin timing.

1. peer   pear peer pear peer pear pear
2. outright   outside outright outdoors outright outside
3. discredit   disobey disorder discredit disobey disorder
4. launch   lunch lurch launch lunch lurch
5. charred   charred chained charred chained char
6. cirrus   circus cirrus circus circle cirrus
7. disc   desk disc disco discs disco
8. credibility   credit credibility credentials credited
9. galactic   galaxy gala galactic galaxy galactic
10. claim   chain chair chain claim clams
11. survey   serve survey service serve survey
12. disturbed   disturb disturbed distress disturb disturbed
13. visible   visual vision visible vision visual
14. craft   crop crafty crusty craft craft
15. meteors   meters meteors meters meaty meteors

TIME: _____

Check each line carefully. Make sure you marked the correct word everytime it appears. Learn any words you may not know.

TOTAL LINES CORRECT: _____

Drill 4

Directions. Follow the same directions as for the previous drill. This time you will be marking the same *phrase* every time it appears on the same line. Again, don't look back on a line, and don't change any errors you may make. Try to finish in thirty-five seconds or less.
Begin timing.

1. sunlight glowing   summer glow   sunlight glare
                           sunlight glowing

2. layers of cold   layers of gold   layers of ice   layers of cold

3. disc-shaped objects   disco objects   disc-shaped objects
                           discs on top

4. peered in   peered into   peered over   peered in
                           peered at

5. flying saucers   flying saucers   flying spoons
                           flying somewhere

6. really believe   readily believe   really brave
                           really believe

7. weather balloons   weather bags   weather balloons
                           whether or not

8. wind currents   wind cuddles   winds cause   wind currents

9. glowing orange   glaring out   glowing orange   glowing red

10. were visible   were variable   were invisible
                           were visible

11. physics professor   physics teacher   physical proof
                           physics professor

12. be justified   be just   being just   be adjusted
                           be justified

13. analyze data   analyze data   analytical data
                           analyze dates

14. strange objects   strange oranges   strange objects
                           straight objects

15. trained observers   trained objects   trained apes
                           trained observers

TIME: _____

Check each line carefully. Make sure you marked the correct phrase everytime it appears. Learn any words you may not know.

TOTAL LINES CORRECT: _____

Drill 5

Directions. Follow the same directions as for the previous drill. Try to finish in thirty-five seconds or less.
Begin timing.

1. former commander   farmer comes   former command
former commander

2. astonished officers   astounded officers   astonished officers
atoned office

3. four indentations   four inventions   four indentations
four interiors

4. they maneuvered   they managed   they magnify
they maneuvered

5. cylindrical object   cylindrical object   cylinders opposite
cylindrical can

6. three occasions   tree occasion   three occasions
three occupied

7. ground control   ground cover   ground coffee
ground control

8. rockets launched   rockets launched   rockets lowered
rockets lifted

9. orbiting Earth   over Earth   orbiting Europe
orbiting Earth

10. space debris   spaced debts   space devil   space debris

11. mass hallucination   mass havoc   mass hallucination
mess halls

12. northern lights   northern tissue   northern turn
northern lights

13. observation craft   observation craft   observe craft
observation crutch

14. natural phenomena   nature phenomena   natural phenomena
nature boy

15. inhabited by   inherit all   interesting buy   inhabited by

TIME: _____

Check each line carefully. Make sure you marked the correct phrase on each line. Learn any words you don't know.

TOTAL LINES CORRECT: _____

R: READING DRILL

A. Reading and Thinking About What You Read

Directions. Before reading the following essay, answer the questions below.

1. Look at the title of the following essay. Do you think the author will

   try to prove UFOs are real? _____ Why? _____

   _____

2. Do you believe there is life in outer space? _____ Why? _____

   _____

   _____

3. What do you think UFOs are? _____

   _____

   _____

Now read the essay. If you come across words you don't know, just keep reading. They will probably make sense as you read on.

UFOs: REAL OR UNREAL?
Robert Kraske

[1] June 24, 1947. As Ken Arnold was flying his small plane near Mount Rainier, Washington, he suddenly peered in disbelief through the windshield. Could he really believe what his eyes told him? Ahead was something that in all his years as a pilot he had never seen before—nine

Excerpted from *Is There Life in Outer Space?* Copyright © 1976 by Robert Kraske. Reprinted by permission of Harcourt Brace Jovanovich, Inc.

gleaming disc-shaped objects, each about 100 feet wide, flying in formation past his line of flight. They were moving fast—about 1,200 m.p.h. he guessed.

[2] Landing at Yakima, Arnold described his strange experience to workers at the field. Someone phoned newspapers and by the following day people across the United States read about "flying saucers," a term coined by a reporter who covered the story.

[3] In the 30 years that have passed since Arnold's "sighting," over 60,000 UFOs have been sighted in the United States alone.

[4] In 1948, the U.S. Air Force began looking into the phenomenon of UFOs. Twenty years later, Air Force investigators had checked into 11,108 UFO sightings. Ninety-four percent or 10,432 turned out to be "misidentifications"—helicopters, jet planes, weather balloons, orbiting space satellites, bright stars, comets, fireballs, meteors, flights of geese, sunlight glowing on ice crystals in cirrus clouds, and mirages caused by light waves bending as they passed through layers of cold and warm air.

[5] A few sightings were outright hoaxes. Two high school boys tied lighted candles to weather balloons and launched them. Wind currents drifted the balloons, glowing orange, across the night sky. Suddenly

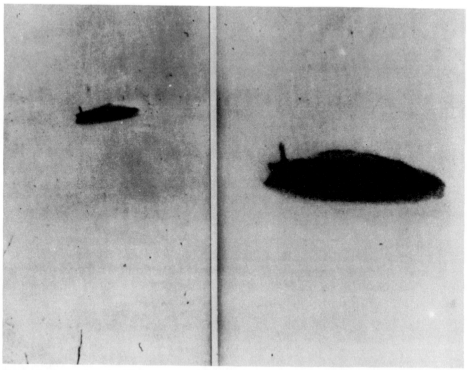

Two photographs of a UFO seen near Detroit (Photograph: Wide World Photos)

each one disappeared in a puff of smoke. Result? People for miles around phoned sheriffs' offices to report UFOs.

[6] Some sightings turned out to be visions of mentally disturbed persons. A Los Angeles woman claimed she had gone for a spin in a UFO with Venusians. She described them as being "unimaginably beautiful." Why hadn't anyone else seen these visitors to Earth? She drew herself up haughtily. They were visible only to "the pure of heart and spirit," she announced.

[7] These misidentifications, hoaxes, and hallucinations tended to discredit UFOs. Who could possibly take them seriously after investigation of thousands of sightings turned up results like these?

[8] In 1968, the director of the Air Force study, Dr. Edward U. Condon, a former physics professor at the University of Colorado, turned in his report. It said in part:

[9] "Careful consideration of the record . . . leads us to conclude that further extensive study of UFOs probably cannot be justified in the expectation that science will be advanced thereby. . . . No direct evidence whatever of a convincing nature now exists for the claim that any UFOs represent spacecraft visiting earth from another civilization."

[10] With the publication of Dr. Condon's report, the Air Force stopped investigating UFO sightings. But not all scientists agreed with the report. The American Institute of Aeronautics and Astronautics, an organization of scientists and engineers, stated that it "did not find a basis in the report . . . that nothing of scientific value will come of further study" of UFOs. The government should continue to collect and analyze data on UFOs, it urged.

[11] And what about the 6 percent or 676 UFO sightings that hadn't been identified by Air Force investigators? Some certainly suggested that strange objects were flying around in our skies. For example:

[12] • While on a train west of Reno, Nevada, a University of Minnesota astronomer saw—in full daylight—a UFO flying parallel with the train just above a ridge of nearby mountains. The craft was visible for four or five minutes, then rose out of sight and disappeared. "I'm familiar with such things as flights of wild geese, balloons, temperature inversions, and the sun shining through the clouds," he said. "I do not suffer from hallucinations. I saw a UFO."

[13] • Over Washington National Airport, five radar operators traced UFOs on three different radar sets. The crafts were moving at speeds from 100 to 800 m.p.h. Four airline pilots, approaching the field for a landing, saw the same luminous objects. This was an example of a sighting made by trained observers, each one independent of the others. None had anything particular to gain from reporting the sighting.

[14] • Two police sergeants in Socorro, New Mexico, investigated a report of a UFO outside town. They saw "a metallic, egg-shaped object" 12 to 15 feet long standing on four short legs in a gulley. As they ap-

proached, bright blue flame spurted from the bottom of the craft, and it rose from the gulley into the sky and sped away. The astonished officers examined the sand and found four indentations each about three and a half inches deep where the metal legs had stood. Bushes around the gulley, they reported, were charred and smoking.

[15] • Entire crowds have also sighted UFOs. At an air show at Longview, Washington, as people watched a sky-writing plane, a UFO appeared, followed by two more. The manager of the show, a former commander in the U.S. Navy, announced the sightings on the public address system. Pilots, engineers, and police officers watched the craft through binoculars. Many reported that they seemed to flutter and waver as they maneuvered over the field. Twenty minutes after the first ones appeared, two more flew up, then all five sped away.

[16] • U.S. astronauts, during the pre-moon flight Gemini tests in 1965, saw UFOs on three occasions.

[17] On the June 3–7 Gemini 4 flight, astronaut James McDivitt reported a long, cylindrical object "white or silver in appearance as seen against the day sky" over the Pacific Ocean with what appeared to be antennas extending from it.

[18] On the next orbit, he radioed: "Just saw a satellite very high . . . just like a star on the ground when you see one go by, a long, long ways away."

[19] Ground control reported no satellites in the area. The nearest satellite, Pegasus, was over 1,200 miles away. Empty fuel tanks from rockets launched before the Gemini flights? On that day, there were ten in space, but at distances from 263 to 587 miles away and unsightable. Besides, the UFO McDivitt had seen was traveling in a south-to-north direction. Satellites and other space debris would be orbiting Earth in an east-to-west direction.

[20] In December, Frank Borman in Gemini 7 reported a "bogey at 10 o'clock high." ("Bogey" is Air Force slang for "unidentified aircraft.")

[21] Ground control replied: "Please check to see if bogey is your booster rocket accompanying you in orbit."

[22] Jim Lovell, in Gemini 7 with Borman, interrupted. "I have the booster on *my* side," he said. "It's a brilliant body in the sun, against the black background" of the sky. He could see it slowly tumbling as it orbited Earth with their spacecraft.

[23] The UFO continued to fly in formation on Borman's side, then suddenly disappeared. The incident took place on the second orbit on the first day of the 14-day Gemini 7 flight.

[24] What did Dr. Condon's report say about the astronauts' three UFO sightings?

[25] "The training . . . of the astronauts put their reports of sightings in the highest category of credibility. Trained to deal in facts only, they avoided personal interpretations of what they saw. The three unexplained sightings . . . are a challenge to the analyst."

The Most Reasonable Explanation

[26] What, then, are UFOs? There are various explanations.

[27] • Some UFOs have been identified as hoaxes and frauds.

[28] • Misidentification of natural phenomena—meteors satellites, fireballs, mirages, etc.—account for some sightings.

[29] • Mass hallucination or "seeing things" may explain some UFOs, but it simply does not provide the answer for cases in which there are visual and radar sightings and cases of simultaneous sightings over a large area by people unknown to each other.

[30] • Secret weapons or secret aircraft might have served as an answer during the first few years of the sightings, but keeping a weapon or aircraft secret over 30 years is not possible. Word would leak out.

[31] Perhaps UFOs are something entirely unknown to us. This view has been expressed best by J. Allen Hynek, Professor of Astronomy at Northwestern University and Director of the Center for UFO Studies in Evanston, Illinois. Testifying before the House Committee on Science and Astronautics of the U.S. Congress in 1968, Dr. Hynek stated that "the UFO problem may not lend itself to an immediate solution in our time. The problem may be far more complex than we imagine. Attempts to solve the problem may be no more productive than attempts to solve the problem of the Aurora Borealis would have been 100 years ago. The cause of the northern lights could not have been determined in the framework of the science of 1868. Scientific knowledge in those days was not sufficient to encompass the phenomenon."

[32] • UFOs may actually be observation craft from other civilizations in space. While scientists recognize that no evidence exists to support this view, there are those who believe it to be the most reasonable explanation for UFOs.

[33] In a newspaper interview, rocket pioneer Dr. Hermann Oberth said: "These objects [UFOs] are conceived and directed by intelligent beings of a very high order. They probably do not originate in our solar system, perhaps not even in our galaxy."

[34] Appearing before the same committee of Congress as Dr. Hynek, the late Dr. James McDonald, a physicist at the University of Arizona, said: "My position is that UFOs are entirely real and we do not know what they are. . . . The possibility that these are extraterrestrial devices, that we are dealing with surveillance from some advanced technology, is a possibility I take very seriously. . . . You have a feeling you are dealing with some very high technology, devices of an entirely real nature which defy explanation in terms of present-day science."

[35] Another scientist, this one from the Westinghouse Astronuclear Laboratory, told the committee: "I have concluded that the earth is being visited by intelligently controlled vehicles whose origin is extraterrestrial. This doesn't mean I know where they come from, why they are here, or how they operate."

A UFO seen in Brazil (Photograph: Wide World Photos)

[36] If, then, we take the last possibility—surveillance by extra-terrestrial beings or spacecraft—as the most reasonable explanation for UFOs, other questions immediately come up.

[37] "Why don't they get in touch with us?" people ask. "Why don't they land right on the White House lawn and declare themselves!"

[38] In reply, scientists say that, while this may be what *we* want, it may not necessarily be what *they* want.

[39] "The most likely explanation, it seems to me," said Dr. Mead, "is that they are simply watching what we are up to—that a responsible society outside our solar system is keeping an eye on us to see that we don't set in motion a chain reaction that might have repercussions far outside our solar system."

[40] "Since the late 1940s," said John W. Macvey, a Fellow of the Royal Astronomical Society, "we have been in possession of dangerous nuclear toys. More recently a 'primitive' capability in space exploration has appeared. To a grand cosmic federation all this might seem faintly ominous. It might seem to constitute a situation worth watching."

[41] A melding of opinions from other scientists might go like this: "Why *should* they want to get in touch with us! We may feel we're more important in the universe and to 'them' than in truth we really are!

They may want to observe us only and not interfere with the development of our civilization. They may not care if we see them; but they also may not care to say 'hello.'

[42] "Thirty years of observation may seem a long time to us, but to them these years may be the same as only a few hours or minutes to us, especially if they measure their life spans in centuries. After all, fruit flies here on earth live only a few days; elephants live over a hundred years. It is possible that life spans of people on Earth and of intelligent creatures on other planets in space would show similar differences."

[43] Some scientists have suggested that Earth is a kind of galactic zoo or wildlife preserve. Just as we set aside wilderness areas and wildlife sanctuaries to allow animals and growing things to develop naturally while we observe them, so perhaps Earth was set aside ages ago for the same purpose.

[44] These scientists say: "The perfect zoo would be one in which the 'specimens' inside do not interact with, and are unaware of, their zookeepers. Nor does the zookeeper make himself known to his charges."

[45] Are we being observed by intelligent beings from other civilizations in the universe? Are they watching our progress in space travel and our use of nuclear weapons? Do we live in a galactic "zoo" observed by our "keepers," but having no communication with them?

[46] Never before in our history have we had to confront ideas like these. The simple fact is that we who have always regarded ourselves as supreme in the universe may not be so. Now we have to recognize that, among the stars in the heavens, there may very well be worlds inhabited by beings who are as superior to us as we are to ants.

B. Comprehension Check

Directions. Answer the following questions. Don't look back at the essay unless the questions tells you to do so.

Recall

1. What is the main idea (thesis) of the essay? _____

    _____

    _____

2. About how long has it been since the first "flying saucer" sighting was reported?
    a. 20 years   c. 40 years
    b. 30 years   d. 50 years

3. How did the term "flying saucer" come about? _____

    _____

    _____

4. T or F. The U.S. Air Force does not believe that UFOs are from outer space.

5. List at least four explanations given to explain what UFOs might be:

    a. _____

    b. _____

    c. _____

    d. _____

Interpretation

6. Scan back to paragraph 3 to answer this question:
    T or F. There have been over 60,000 UFOs sighted throughout the world over the past 30 years.

7. Scan back to paragraphs 20–22 to answer this question:
    T or F. Both Lovell and Borman saw a UFO when orbiting Earth in Gemini 7.

8. Why do some scientists suggest that Earth is a "kind of galactic zoo"? _____

_____

9. Scan back to paragraph 40 to answer this question:

What is meant by the phrase "a grand cosmic federation"? To whom

or what is Macvey referring? _____

_____

_____

Application

10. Based on what you know and what you have just read, explain why you do or do not believe some UFOs are manned by creatures from space. _____

_____

_____

_____

_____

E: EXERCISES IN VOCABULARY

A. Drills

Drill 1: Word Categories (Part A)

Directions. Below are two lists of words. Write the letter of the word from the right-hand column in the blank in front of the word by the number that means the same thing or almost the same thing.

_____ 1. hallucination   a. trick

_____ 2. protagonist   b. expose

_____ 3. hoax   c. delusion

_____ 4. mentor   d. stuck-up

_____ 5. tote   e. bright

_____ 6. botch   f. hero

_____ 7. discredit   g. lookout

_____ 8. haughty   h. wreck

_____ 9. luminous   i. carry

_____ 10. surveillance   j. teacher

Check your answers:
1. c,   2. f,   3. a,   4. j,   5. i,   6. h,   7. b,   8. d,   9. e,   10. g.

Part B

Directions. Below are a list of words and an unfinished outline. Complete the outline on the next page by writing the words from the list in the correct category.

weapons	comedy	guard	armor
luminous	fort	sparkling	wittiness
astronauts	satellites	orbit	clear
joking	intelligent	levity	clown

I. defense

    A. _____

    B. _____

    C. _____

    D. _____

II. humor

    A. _____

    B. _____

    C. _____

    D. _____

    E. _____

III. bright

    A. _____

    B. _____

    C. _____

    D. _____

IV. space

    A. _____

    B. _____

    C. _____

Check your answers. Your list of words can be in any order as long as they appear in the right group.
Group I: weapons, fort, guard, armor.
Group II: joking, comedy, levity, wittiness.
Group III: luminous, sparkling, clear, intelligent.
Group IV: astronauts, satellites, orbit.

Drill 2: Greek Word Parts

Directions. In the last chapter you learned some Greek word parts. Study the Greek word parts below. Review the ones in the last chapter if you need to. Then answer the questions that follow.

anthrop = man
derm = skin
path = feeling, disease
phil = love
phob = fear
psych = mind
zo = animal

aster (astro) = star
bibl = book
dem = people
crat, cracy = power, rule
gam = marriage
miso, mis = hatred
pseudo = false

1. If biology is the study of life, what is *anthropology?* _____

    _____

2. If *a* means without, what does *apathy* mean? _____

    _____

3. What is *astrology?* _____

    _____

4. What is a *philanthropist?* _____

    _____

5. What word means the study of the mind? _____

    _____

6. If *phobia* means fear of, what does *anthropophobia* mean? _____

    _____

7. What does *democracy* mean? _____

    _____

8. What word means the study of animals? _____

    _____

9. What would *galactic zoology* refer to? _____

_____

10. If *graph* means writing or record, what is a *bibliography*? _____

_____

11. What is a *misogamist?* _____

_____

12. If *nym* means name, what is a *pseudonym?* _____

_____

13. What is a *pseudopsychologist?* _____

_____

14. What is a *bibliophile?* _____

_____

15. If *poly* means many, what is *polygamy?* _____

_____

16. What word means the opposite of *philanthropist?* _____

_____

17. What word means the study of skin disorders? _____

_____

18. What is the opposite of a *philogamist?* _____

_____

19. What is *pseudoscience?* _____

_____

20. What is the opposite of a *misanthrope?* _____

_____

Check your answers with these:
1. the study of man or mankind, 2. without feeling or showing no feeling,
3. the study of the stars, 4. a person who loves people or mankind,
5. psychology, 6. fear of man, 7. people power or rule by the people,
8. zoology, 9. study of animals in the galaxy, 10. literally, book record;
actually a list of books, 11. a person who hates marriage, 12. false name,
13. false or phoney psychologist, 14. lover of books, 15. many marriages,
usually at the same time, 16. misanthrope, 17. dermatology (notice the
added letters), 18. misogamist, 19. false science, 20. philanthropist

Drill 3: Latin Word Parts

Directions. Here are some more Latin word parts. Study them, and
then answer the questions that follow.

aud, audit = hear, listen to	*cred* = believe
dic (t) = tell, speak	*fort* = strong
mit, miss = send, sent	*gen* = race, birth, kind
ped, pod = foot	*contra* = against
fac = make, do	*cap* = take, hold
man, manu = hand	*de* = down from, reverse

1. If you have an *auditory* problem, what kind of problem is it? _____

   _____

2. If you *contradict* someone's story, what are you doing? _____

   _____

3. If you did not know what *manufacture* means, how could you fig-

   ure it out? _____

   _____

4. What does it mean to *transmit* something? _____

   _____

5. If *credible* means believable, what does *incredible* mean?

   _____

6. If you say someone has *fortitude* when it comes to not eating too
   much, what does it mean?

   _____

7. Why do you think the first book in the Bible is called *Genesis?*

_____

8. If an actress *captivates* an audience, what does it mean?

_____

9. If someone gives you an *audition,* what are they giving you?

_____

10. If *tri* means three, what is a *tripod?*

_____

11. To do something *manually* is to do it by _____

12. *Genes* have to do with _____

_____

13. *Pedal, pedestrian, peds*—all have the root _____, which means

_____

_____

14. When you *deplane,* you are _____

_____

15. When you give *credence* to someone's story, you _____

_____

16. Circle the Latin roots in the following words:
    a. auditorium   c. dictation
    b. factory   d. captive

Check your answers with these:
1. hearing problem, 2. saying something against them, 3. *manu* means "hand" and *fac* means "to make" or "to make by hand,"   4. send across, such as transmit a message by telegram, 5. not believable, 6. strong will power, 7. *gen* means "birth" and *Genesis* discusses the birth of Earth,   8. capture or

please them,   9. a chance to try out; they will listen to you,   10. three-legged stand, such as a camera tripod,   11. hand,   12. race or kind of skin, hair, eye color, and so on,   13. ped/foot,   14. getting off the plane,   15. support it; believe it,   16. (a) aud (b) fac (c) dic (d) cap.

Drill 4: Root Words

Directions. Below are some phrases in groups. In each group, three of the four phrases have words that are from the same root word. Fill in the root word, and check the blank in front of the phrase that does *not* have a word from the same root.
For example:

    a _____ a portable TV

    b ✓ portray a villain

    c _____ good transportation

    d _____ import tax

    Root: *port*

1. a. _____ having countless bills

    b. _____ needs to recount

    c. _____ hilly country

    d. _____ he miscounted

    Root: _____

2. a. _____ a new automobile

    b. _____ what the mob wants

    c. _____ it's very mobile

    d. _____ let's mobilize now

    Root: _____

3. a. _____ no longer manufactures

    b. _____ not on factory time

    c. _____ those aren't facts

    d. _____ manufacturing sandals

    Root: _____

4. a. _____ throw the dice

    b. _____ a little dictator

    c. _____ take dictation

    d. _____ has good diction

    Root: _____

5. a. _____ she captivated him

   b. _____ they captured four

   c. _____ take no captives

   d. _____ six or seven caps

   Root: _____

6. a. _____ telephone

   b. _____ he's a phony

   c. _____ phonograph record

   d. _____ study of phonics

   Root: _____

Check your answers with these:
1. c; root: *count,* 2. b; root: *mob,* 3. c; root: fac, 4. a; root: *dic,* 5. d; root: *cap,* 6. b; root: *phon.*

Drill 5: Words in Context

Directions. Below is a passage from the essay you read in this chapter. Read it and fill in the blanks with the words you think fit. Don't look back at the essay.

"Thirty years of observation may seem a long time to us, but to them these years may be the same as only a few hours or minutes to us, especially if they measure (1) _____ life spans in centuries. (2) _____ all, fruit flies here

(3) _____ earth live only a

(4) _____ days; elephants live over

(5) _____ hundred years. It is

(6) _____ that life spans of

(7) _____ on Earth and of

(8) _____ creatures on other planets

(9) _____ space would show similar

(10) _____."

Some scientists have suggested (11) _____

Earth is a kind (12) _____ galactic zoo or

wildlife (13) _____. Just as we set

(14) _____ wilderness areas and wildlife

(15) _____ to allow animals and

(16) _____ things to develop naturally

(17) _____ we observe them, so

(18) _____ Earth was set aside

(19) _____ ago for the same

(20) _____.

These scientists say: "The (21) _____ zoo

would be on (22) _____ which the 'specimens'

inside (23) _____ not interact with, and

(24) _____unaware of, their zookeepers.

(25) _____ does the zookeeper make

(26) _____ known to his charges."

(27) _____ we being observed by

(28) _____ beings from other civilizations

(29) _____ our universe? Are they

(30) _____ our progress in space

(31) _____ and our use of

(32) _____ weapons? Do we live

(33) _____ a galactic "zoo" observed

(34) _____ our "keepers," but having

(35) _____ communication with them?

Never (36) _____ in our history have

(37) _____ had to confront ideas

(38) _____ these. The simple fact

(39) _____ that we who have

(40) _____ regarded ourselves as supreme

(41) _____ the universe may not

(42) _____ so. Now we have

(43) _____ recognize that, among the

(44) _____ in the heavens, there

(45) _____ very well be worlds

(46) _____ be beings who are

(47) _____ superior to us as

(48) _____ are to ants. Are

(49) _____ real? What do you

(50) _____?

Check your answers with these:
1. their, 2. After, 3. on, 4. few, 5. a, 6. possible, 7. people,
8. intelligent, 9. in, 10. differences, 11. that, 12. of, 13. preserve,
14. aside, 15. sanctuaries, 16. growing, 17. while, 18. perhaps, 19. ages,
20. purpose, 21. perfect, 22. in, 23. do, 24. are, 25. Nor, 26. himself,
27. Are, 28. intelligent, 29. in, 30. watching, 31. travel, 32. nuclear,
33. in, 34. by, 35. no, 36. before, 37. we, 38. like, 39. is, 40. always,
41. in, 42. be, 43. to, 44. stars, 45. may, 46. inhabited, 47. as,
48. we, 49. UFOs, 50. think.

B. Vocabulary Check

Part A

Directions. Write a sentence using each of the following words correctly.
You may change endings if necessary.

1. hallucination: _____

   _____

2. hoax: _____

   _____

3. tote: _____

   _____

4. botch: _____

   _____

5. discredit: _____

   _____

6. haughtily: _____

   _____

7. luminous: _____

   _____

8. discredit: _____

   _____

9. surveillance: _____

   _____

10. mentor: _____

_____

Part B

Directions. Define the following words.

1. phobia: _____

2. astrology: _____

3. democracy: _____

4. anthropology: _____

5. zoology: _____

6. credible: _____

7. contradict: _____

8. captivate: _____

9. deplane: _____

10. credence: _____

Part C

Directions. Supply the word that fits the following definitions.

1. to do by hand   _____

2. a person walking   _____

3. to send a message   _____

4. a place to hear speakers

   and concerts   _____

5. believable   _____

6. a book lover   _____

7. a phony lover   _____

8. many marriages   _____

9. someone who hates man _____

10. a list of books   _____

P: PERFECTING READING SKILLS

A. Comprehending Reference Materials

Drill 1: The Table of Contents

Directions. A table of contents appears in the front of nearly every book. It is a table or list of the book's contents. By skimming a book's table of contents, you get a good idea what the book will cover. A table of contents appears on page 302. First, *skim* over the table of contents. Then answer each of the following questions below by *scanning* the table of contents for the answer.

1. Can you tell from skimming and scanning if the book takes seriously

   UFOs? _____ Why? _____

   _____

2. If you did not know what is meant by "Close Encounters of the Third

   Kind," where could you find an answer? _____

   _____

   _____

3. If you were going to write a paper on the history of UFOs, would

   this book contain any information to help you? _____ Where?

   _____

   _____

4. What type of photographs are in the book? _____

   _____

5. If you wanted to read more about UFOs, is there anything in the

book to help you? _____ Where? _____

_____

6. On what page would you find out about scientists' attitudes about

UFOs? _____

7. On what page would you find out about the Air Force's Blue Book?

_____

8. If you started reading on page 141, what would you learn about?

_____

_____

9. By just reading the titles to the three parts of the book, what can

you guess the book will cover? _____

_____

_____

10. If you were doing a report on UFOs, would this book be helpful?

_____ Why? _____

_____

Contents

Drill 2: The Index

Directions. An index appears at the end of a book. An index lists in alphabetical order the subjects, names, and terms used in the book. Page numbers are given so you can easily find something or see if the book covers what you are looking for. Part of an index is shown on page 304. Scan the index to answer the following questions.

1. On what pages would you find information about "Close Encounters of the Second Kind"? _____

2. On what page would you find information about a "Close Encounter of the Second Kind" in Canada? _____

3. Does the book have any information on UFO sightings by astronauts?

   _____

4. Is there some coverage in the book on Air Force Blue Book cases?

   _____

5. Was there a report of a "Close Encounter of the Third Kind" in New Guinea? _____

6. What does ATIC stand for? _____

   _____

7. If you wanted to know what the Condon Committee was, where would you look? _____

8. Pretend you had to read the first eighty-three pages of this book. Tomorrow you are going to have a test on those pages. Scan the index for all listings from page 1 to page 83. What subjects, names, or terms would you need to review before the test? _____

   _____

   _____

9. How can what you did with question 8 above help you in preparing for exams in other classes? _____

_____

_____

_____

Index

Drill 3: Glossaries

Directions. A glossary is a short dictionary of words and terms used in the book you are reading. Not all books have glossaries. Usually, such books as history texts, psychology texts, chemistry texts, and so on, or books dealing with special subjects have glossaries. You can save a trip to the dictionary when a book has a glossary. Many words are usually defined as they are used in the context of the book. Scan the partial glossary on page 306 to answer the following questions.

1. What subject does the book from which this glossary is taken deal

   with? _____

   How do you know? _____

2. What is the difference between the Earth's equator and a celestial

   equator? _____

   _____

   _____

3. What is a constellation? _____

   _____

   _____

4. How does a constellation differ from a galaxy? _____

   _____

   _____

   _____

5. How far does light travel in a year? _____

   _____

6. What is an astronomical unit? _____

   _____

7. What's the average distance of the earth from the sun? _____

_____

8. How can a glossary be helpful to you? _____

_____

_____

Glossary of Terms

apastron The point of greatest distance of separation of two stars circling each other.

astronomical unit The average distance of earth from the sun; about 150,000,000 kilometers.

atom A particle of matter made up of a central nucleus surrounded by electrons.

atomic nucleus A small structure at the center of an atom, containing nearly all the mass of the atom.

axis of rotation The imaginary straight line about which an object spins.

binary stars Two stars that are close together in space and that revolve about each other.

celestial equator An imaginary circle about the sky, lying exactly above every point on earth's equator.

celestial poles Imaginary points in the sky that are directly above earth's North and South Poles.

constellation A grouping of stars in the sky, often pictured in some familiar shape (the Big and Little Dippers.)

double stars Two stars that appear to be close together in the sky.

galaxy A huge collection of millions and trillions of stars (our sun is a part of a galaxy).

light-year The distance light travels in a year, about 9,500,000,000,000 kilometers.

Drill 4: Bibliographies

Directions. A bibliography, as you learned in the vocabulary section, is a list of books that can be used to find more information about a subject. Often, bibliographies appear at the end of chapters or at the end of a book. A bibliography appears on page 308. Scan it to find the answers to the questions below.

1. What subject does this bibliography cover? _____

   _____

2. Is this bibliography a fairly recent list of books on the subject?

   _____ How do you know? _____

   _____

3. If you wanted to read more about galaxies, what are the names of the

   books that probably would be most helpful? _____

   _____

   _____

   _____

4. Which of the following is the correct way the bibliography is written?
   Circle one.
   a. Publisher, title, author, date.
   b. Title, author, publisher, date.
   c. Author, title, publisher, date.
   d. None of the above.

5. Why do you suppose there is no author's name for the second book

   listing? _____

   _____

6. What publisher has more than one book on the list? _____

   _____

7. Why are Isaac Asimov's books listed first? _____

_____

8. Which of the books on the list would probably be best for someone who

did not know much about astronomy? _____

_____

Bibliography

Asimov, Isaac. *Alpha Centauri*. Lothrop, Lee & Shepard Company, 1976.

————. *To the Ends of the Universe*. Revised Edition. Walker and Company, 1976.

Bok, B. J., and P. F. Bok. *The Milky Way*, 4th edition. Harvard University Press, 1974.

Cleminshaw, C. H. *The Beginner's Guide to the Stars*. Thomas Y. Crowell Company, 1977.

Field, George B., et al. *The Redshift Controversy*. W. A. Benjamin Co., 1973.

Hoyle, Fred. *Astronomy and Cosmology*. W. H. Freeman & Co., 1973.

Hynek, J. Allen. *The UFO Experience*. Henry Regnery Co., 1972.

Mitton, Simon. *Exploring the Galaxies*. Charles Scribner's Sons, 1976.

Shapley, Harlow. *Galaxies*, 3d edition. Harvard University Press, 1972.

Whitney, Charles A. *The Discovery of Our Galaxy*. Angus and Robertson, 1972.

B. Comprehending Maps, Tables, and Graphs

Drill 1: Reading Maps

Problem. At 5:45 P.M. on April, 24, 1964, a "Close Encounter of the Third Kind" occurred in Socorro, New Mexico, which lasted between five and ten minutes. A Socorro policeman, Lonnie Zamora, was chasing a speeding car south of town. The speeding car escaped when officer Zamora saw a descending object that was spouting flames and making explosive noises. The craft landed, and he saw two white-cloaked figures. Shortly after, the craft took off and disappeared. It left burn marks on the ground where it landed.

Use the map on page 311 to answer the following questions.

1. If Zamora did see an alien space ship, what is near Socorro that

   would be of interest to creatures from outer space? _____

   _____

2. Is Albuquerque north or south of Socorro? _____

3. If you were in Las Vegas and wanted to drive to the spot where the spacecraft is supposed to have landed, what would be the fastest

   route to get there? _____

   _____

4. About how far is Socorro from Lincoln National Forest? _____

   _____

5. Which is closer to Socorro, Albuquerque or Las Cruces? _____

   _____

6. Which city is farthest east of Socorro?
   a. Tucumcari   b. Roswell   c. Artesia

7. What highway goes from Alamogordo to Tucumcari? _____

   _____

8. What highway runs through the Apache Indian Reservation? _____

   _____

9. On what highways was the speeding car that Officer Zamora was

   chasing probably traveling? _____

   _____

10. What is the first highway the driver of the speeding car could turn

    off? _____

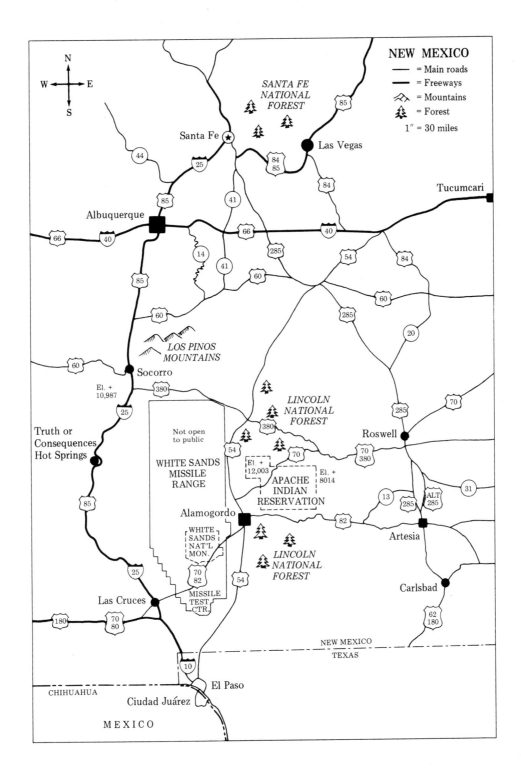

NEW MEXICO

— = Main roads
━ = Freeways
⌃⌃ = Mountains
🌲 = Forest

1″ = 30 miles

SANTA FE
NATIONAL
FOREST

Santa Fe ★

Las Vegas

Tucumcari

Albuquerque

66   40

66

40

44

25

85

84
85

84

41

14

285

54

84

41

60

60

285

60

20

LOS PINOS
MOUNTAINS

Socorro

60

El. +
10,987

380

25

LINCOLN
NATIONAL
FOREST

380

Roswell

285

70

Truth or
Consequences
Hot Springs

WHITE SANDS
MISSILE
RANGE

Not open
to public

54

70

70
380

El. +
12,003

APACHE
INDIAN
RESERVATION

El. +
8014

13

285

ALT
285

31

85

Alamogordo

82

Artesia

WHITE
SANDS
NAT'L
MON.

LINCOLN
NATIONAL
FOREST

25

70
82

54

Carlsbad

Las Cruces

MISSILE
TEST
CTR.

NEW MEXICO
TEXAS

62
180

180

70
80

10

CHIHUAHUA

El Paso

Ciudad Juárez

MEXICO

Drill 2: Reading Tables

Directions. Tables, charts, and graphs are used to show information that is easier to find visually than in paragraph form. A table or chart is arranged to make it possible to find quickly specific facts, to compare information, and to show relationships. For instance, look at the table on page 313. Notice that it gives information on "Close Encounters with UFOs of the First Kind." The table is divided into five columns. Use the table to scan for the answers to the questions below.

1. How many years does the table cover? _____

2. What is the longest length of sighting listed in the table? _____

3. What is the shortest length of sighting listed? _____

   _____

4. Where did a UFO sighting occur that the largest number of people

   saw? _____

5. Did more sightings occur during A.M. or P.M.? _____

6. What year has the most sightings listed? _____

7. What state has had more than one "Close Encounter of the First

   Kind"? _____

8. Are the sightings listed in Table 1 the only ones that occurred be-

   tween 1954 and 1967? _____

   How do you know? _____

9. What is meant by 2 + 1 + 1 observers? _____

   _____

10. Why are there no listings after 1969? _____

    _____

Table 1

Major UFO Encounters of the First Kind
Recorded by the Air Force** (1954–1967)

Date	Time	Place	No. of Observers	Length of Sighting
8–20–55	10:45 P.M.	Kenora, Ont.	2	4 mins
6–26–63	1:00 A.M.	Weymouth, Mass.	2	1 min
4–3–64	9:00 P.M.	Monticello, Wis.	3	5–10 mins
3–8–65	7:40 P.M.	Mt. Airy, Md.	3	3 mins
6–19–65	4:00 A.M.	Rocky, Okla.	2	2–3 mins
1–11–66	7:40 P.M.	Meyerstown, Pa.	4	10 mins
2–6–66	6:05 A.M.	Nederland, Tex.	3	5 mins
4–17–66	5:05 A.M.	Portage County, Ohio	*2+1+1	1 hr 35 mins
4–22–66	9:00 P.M.	Beverly, Mass.	10	30 mins
7–22–66	11:30 P.M.	Freemont, Ind.	2	5–8 mins
10–10–66	5:20 P.M.	Newton, Ill.	6	3–4 mins
4–17–67	9:00 P.M.	Jefferson City, Mo.	*1+1+2	10–15 mins
10–14–67	2:30 A.M.	Mendota, Ca.	3	3 mins
10–27–67	3:05 A.M.	Parshall, N.D.	*1+1	5 mins

(There are many other sightings not listed here)

*Refers to separate groups or individual observers.
**The Air Force stopped recording UFO sightings after 1969.

Drill 3: Reading Graphs

Directions: Graphs can be drawn in several ways: bar graphs, line graphs, and circle graphs. Which type is used depends on which form can best explain the information being presented. Use the graphs on pages 315 and 316 to answer the following questions.

1. Which is the largest planet in diameter?

   _____

2. Which is the smallest?

   _____

3. Which planet is the closest to the sun?

   _____

4. Which planet is the farthest from the sun?

   _____

5. Which is closer to the sun, Uranus or Earth?

   _____

6. How many planets are closer to the sun than Earth?

   _____

7. How many planets are smaller than Earth?

   _____

8. About how many miles in diameter is Earth?

   _____

9. How far away from the sun is Earth?

   _____

10. Which planet is the coldest and why?

    _____

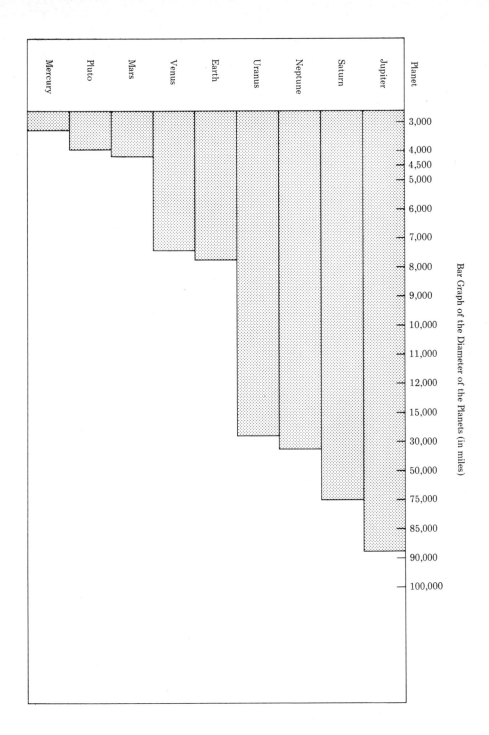

Bar Graph of the Diameter of the Planets (in miles)

Planet	
Jupiter	
Saturn	
Neptune	
Uranus	
Earth	
Venus	
Mars	
Pluto	
Mercury	

3,000
4,000
4,500
5,000
6,000
7,000
8,000
9,000
10,000
11,000
12,000
15,000
30,000
50,000
75,000
85,000
90,000
100,000

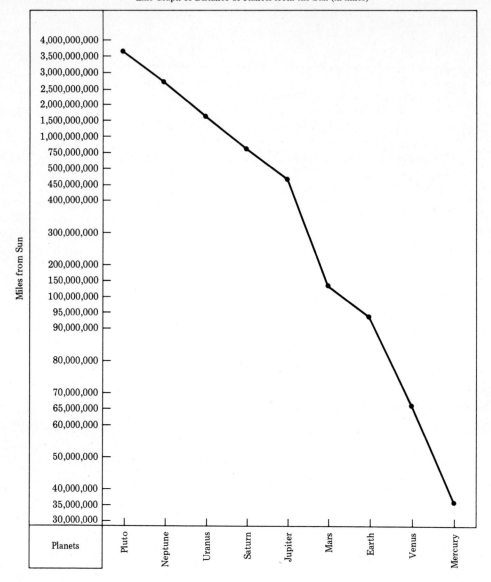

C. Comprehending This Chapter

Directions. As a review of this chapter, answer these questions and be able to discuss them in class.

1. What words from the beginning of this chapter (p. 270) do you need to review or discuss?

2. Name at least six Greek word parts discussed in this chapter. Name six words that contain them.
3. Name at least six Latin word parts discussed in this chapter. Name six words that contain them.
4. Define the following: table of contents, index, glossary, bibliography, tables, graphs.
5. Explain skimming and scanning.
6. What, if any, problems did you have in this chapter?
7. What did you learn or relearn from working in this chapter?
8. "I consider a visit to our planet by an extraterrestrial race to be extremely probable."—Hermann Oberth, pioneer of modern rocketry What do you think?

UNIT 3
CHECK TEST (Chapters 7–9)

Part 1: Word Knowledge

A. *Directions.* Below are two columns. Write the letter of the synonym in column B in the blank by the number.

A	B
1. _____ fad	a. odor
2. _____ aroma	b. unlawful
3. _____ expensive	c. craze
4. _____ illegal	d. enough
5. _____ sufficient	e. costly

B. *Directions.* Below are two columns. Write the letter of the antonym in column B in the blank by the number.

A	B
1. _____ safe	a. enter
2. _____ expensive	b. lacking
3. _____ leave	c. dangerous
4. _____ permit	d. prevent
5. _____ sufficient	e. cheap

C. *Directions.* Define the following word parts.

1. tele: _____

2. micro: _____

3. graph: _____

4. ology: _____

5. auto: _____

6. geo: _____

7. bio: _____

8. scope: _____

9. and: _____

10. cred: _____

11. gen: _____

12. ped, pod: _____

13. manu: _____

14. meter: _____

15. contra: _____

Part 2: Word Usage

Directions. Below are two columns. In the blank by the word in the first column, write in the letter of the definition from the second column.

1. _____ imitating   a. brave, fearless

2. _____ colleagues   b. know-how, experience

3. _____ demoralize   c. fellow workers

4. _____ neurotic   d. to stare

5. _____ bigot   e. far-reaching, broad

6. _____ savoir faire   f. overly proud manner

7. _____ intrepid   g. nervous

8. ____ peer

9. ____ haughtily

10. ____ discredit

11. ____ extensive

12. ____ luminous

13. ____ justified

14. ____ debris

15. ____ surveillance

h. proved to be right, free from guilt

i. copying

j. remains, ruins

k. act of watchfulness, observation

l. biased person

m. to prove false

n. disturb, weaken

o. bright, clear

Part 3: Reading Comprehension

Directions. (1) Scan the following article for answers to the questions below. (2) Next read the article. (3) Then answer the questions following the article.

Scanning Questions

1. Skim over the first paragraph and read the headings. Then write a statement that tells what the article is about. _____

   _____

   _____

2. How many steps to this technique are there? _____

   _____

HOW TO STUDY READ

Most students don't know how to study read. They usually open their textbook to the assigned page and start reading. But before long their minds have wandered off somewhere. Or they read and mark up the pages by underlining everything that seems important. Study reading is different from regular reading. You are expected to remember more and, in most cases, will be tested on what you read. Here is a four-step method for study reading textbooks that can help improve comprehension and promote longer retention of what is read.

Step One: Prepare to Read

It's important to prepare yourself to read. Much time can be lost when you try to plunk yourself into reading an assigned chapter if your mind isn't ready. Because you can think faster than you can read, your mind can easily go into daydreams or other thoughts if you aren't ready to read an assignment. The wisest thing to do is to skim over the chapter to be read. Let the title sink in. Read an opening paragraph or two to see what the chapter is about. Then read the headings and subheadings. Next read the summary or the last couple of paragraphs. It may not make a lot of sense, but your mind will begin to clear out other thoughts. You'll begin to think about the content of the chapter. If there are study questions at the end of the chapter, read those. Having questions about what you are reading helps concentration and gives you a purpose for reading.

Step Two: Read

After you have looked over the chapter, you are ready to read. If you don't have any questions about the content of the chapter, make some up. You can do this by turning the title and headings into questions. If you are reading a long chapter, don't try to read too much at once. It's better if you read from one heading to the next. Then stop and follow Step Three below. If there are no headings in the chapter, read about two pages; then stop and follow Step Three below.

Step Three: Examine What You Read

By reading only short passages and then stopping, you stand a better chance of concentrating on the chapter's content. The third step is now to examine what you read. Put the textbook aside, and write some notes in your own words. In a few key words or phrases, write down the major points you just read. Research shows that doing this aids comprehension and retention for future tests. If you don't believe in taking reading notes, at least try to recite to yourself the key points you just read. When you are satisfied you understand what you read, then read from the next heading to the next, stopping every once in a while to take notes or go over what you read. Follow this step until you are finished with the chapter. Though this may seem slow, as you practice this study reading technique, you'll discover it's really faster because you don't waste time with losing concentration or having to reread what you've read.

Step Four: Plan to Review

This last step does not take place immediately after you read, but it's very important for remembering what you read and can mean the difference between a *C* and an *A* on a test. You should make a definite plan to review your reading notes every week. As you move through a course, you have more and more to learn. You can't remember it all. In fact, unless we review every week what has been studied before, we can forget over 80 percent of what we read. So plan to review once a week. Go over your notes. If they don't make sense when you review, go back to the chapter and reread what isn't clear. (It's important to write chapter titles and page references to key points in your notes so you can find things quickly when you review.)

Research shows it's not so much how long you study that gets good grades, but how well and how often you study. Try this four-step method (PREP) and watch those grades go up.

Now answer these questions. Try not to look back unless you have to do so.

3. T or F.   Study reading is different from regular reading because we are expected to remember more and be prepared to take tests.
4. T or F.   It is important to prepare ourselves to study read because otherwise our minds may wander and we may waste time rereading passages.

5. What is Step One? _____

_____

6. What is Step Two? _____

_____

7. What is Step Three? _____

_____

8. What is Step Four? _____

_____

9. If we don't review what we have read at least once a week or once every two weeks, research shows we can forget as much as _____ percent of what we read.

10. Research shows it's not so much how long we study that gets good grades, but _____

_____

Comprehension Record Chart

Directions. Write in the blanks the number of comprehension questions you got correct for each of three comprehension sections.

Chapter	Essay Title	Comprehension Scores		
		Recall	Interpretation	Application
1	Stevie Wonder	___ of 2	___ of 3	___ of 1
2	. . . the Real Dracula . . .	___ of 4	___ of 3	___ of 2
3	My Son, the Mechanic	___ of 4	___ of 4	___ of 2
4	Jobs and Personalities	___ of 6	___ of 2	___ of 1
5	The Great Babe	___ of 4	___ of 3	___ of 2
6	Butchering at Wounded Knee	___ of 4	___ of 3	___ of 2
7	Puff, Puff . . . Cigarette	___ of 4	___ of 4	___ of 2
8	Shape Up, Bionic Woman	___ of 4	___ of 4	___ of 2
9	UFOs	___ of 5	___ of 4	___ of 1

Unit Review Test Scores Chart

Directions: Record the results of each unit test in the correct blanks.

Unit 1
Part 1: Word Knowledge _____ correct of 25 items
Part 2: Word Usage _____ correct of 15 items
Part 3: Reading Comprehension _____ correct of 8 items

Self-evaluation: In the space below write a brief self-evaluation on how well you think you are doing, what you need to review, and what you could do to improve your scores.

Unit 2
Part 1: Word Knowledge _____ correct of 25 items
Part 2: Word Usage _____ correct of 15 items
Part 3: Reading Comprehension _____ correct of 10 items

Self-evaluation: In the space below write a brief self-evaluation on how well you think you are doing, what you need to review, and what you could do to improve your scores.

Unit 3
Part 1: Word Knowledge _____ correct of 25 items
Part 2: Word Usage _____ correct of 15 items
Part 3: Reading Comprehension _____ correct of 10 items

Self-evaluation: In the space below write a brief self-evaluation on how well you think you are doing, what you need to review, and what you could do to improve your scores.

NAME _____ SECTION _____ DATE _____

ADDITIONAL READINGS

The following articles do not have vocabulary or comprehension drills. Use them to read for pleasure. Apply the skills you are learning when you read them. The subject and content of the articles are similar to some of the articles in other chapters, but they each have something different to say or think about.

TEXTBOOKS AND THE AMERICAN INDIAN

On December 1, 1927, the Grand Council Fire of American Indians presented a memorial to the mayor of Chicago.

[1] You tell all white men "America First." We believe in that. We are the only ones, truly, that are 100 percent. We therefore ask you while you are teaching school children about America, first, teach them truth about the First Americans.

[2] We do not know if school histories are pro-British, but we do know that they are unjust to the left of our people—the American Indian. They call all white victories, battles, and all Indian victories, massacres. The battle with Custer has been taught to school children as a fearful massacre on our part. We ask that this, as well as other incidents, be told fairly. If the Custer battle was a massacre, what was Wounded Knee?

[3] History books teach that Indians were murderers—is it murder to fight in self-defense? Indians killed white men because white men took their lands, ruined their hunting grounds, burned their forests, destroyed their buffalo. White men penned our people on reservations, then took away the reservations. White men who rise to protect their property are called patriots—Indians who do the same are called murderers.

[4] White men call Indians treacherous—but no mention is made of broken treaties on the part of the white man. . . .

[5] White men called Indians thieves—and yet we lived in frail skin lodges and needed no locks or iron bars. White men call Indians savages. What is civilization? Its marks are a noble religion and philosophy, original arts, stirring music, rich story and legend. We had these. . . .

[6] We sang songs that carried in their melodies all the sounds of nature—the running of waters, the sighing of winds, and the calls of the

From Rupert Costo, ed., *Textbooks and the American Indian* (San Francisco: The American Indian Historical Society, 1975). Reprinted by permission.

animals. Teach these to your children that they may come to love nature as we love it.

[7] We had our statesmen—and their oratory has never been equalled. Teach the children some of these speeches of our people, remarkable for their brilliant oratory.

[8] We played games—games that brought good health and sound bodies. Why not put these in your schools? We told stories. Why not teach school children more of the wholesome proverbs and legends of our people? Tell them how we loved all that was beautiful. That we killed game only for food, not for fun. Indians think white men who kill for fun are murderers.

[9] Tell your children of the friendly acts of Indians to the white people who first settled here. Tell them of our leaders and heroes and their deeds. . . . Put in your history books the Indian's part in the World War. Tell how the Indian fought for a country of which he was not a citizen, for a flag to which he had no claim, and for a people that have treated him unjustly.

[10] We ask this, Chief, to keep sacred the memory of our people.

TEENAGERS AND ALCOHOL

[1] A violent banging on the front door at 2 A.M. brings Mrs. Southerby rushing down the stairs in her robe. She's been tossing and fuming in bed because Sally, her 16-year-old, should have been in at midnight. As Mrs. Southerby opens the door, Sally lurches toward her, grinning stupidly.

[2] "I cud'n get th' key t' fit," Sally mumbles thickly. Her hair is tangled, her clothes rumpled, and she smells of vomit. "I'm gonna be sick agin," she says as she crumples to the floor.

[3] Mr. Southerby appears to see what the commotion is. He helps Sally to her feet, and as he tries to lead her down the hallway, he catches the strong odor of beer from her breath. He says to his wife, "She'll be all right, Ellen, she's just drunk."

[4] Mrs. Southerby sighs with relief, "Thank God it isn't drugs!"

[5] Scenes like this one are happening all across the country. Alcohol, the number one national drug problem, has hit a new high among young people. Reports from recent studies by the U.S. Commission on Marijuana and Drug Abuse show that by the age of 14, seven out of ten young people have had their first drink of alcohol. By the age of 16, the number of teenage drinkers reaches the level of 87 percent.

[6] The rise in teenage drinking has also been noted by officials at Alcoholics Anonymous. A.A. groups all across the country are now scheduling more than double the number of youth-oriented meetings than they held a year ago.

[7] What accounts for this all-time high in teenage drinking? Social workers, sociologists, and public officials suggest a number of reasons:

[8] • Radio and TV advertising of beer and pop wine, such as strawberry wine and apple wine, on teen-oriented shows. These wines have more appeal for younger drinkers than for adults.

[9] • Easy availability of alcohol, as well as low price compared with other drugs. "Most grocery stores will sell you beer or wine without checking your ID," Mike T., a junior from a Virginia high school, told us. "Besides, if you can't buy, there's always the old man's liquor cabinet to rip off."

[10] • The legal crackdown on marijuana and other drugs classified as narcotics. "Marijuana is too expensive and you're more likely to get arrested," comments a Los Angeles teenager, Alex R.

[11] • The lowering of the drinking age to 18 in many states. With friends in the 18-year-old age bracket who can buy alcohol legally, the 15- to 17-year-olds have easier access to liquor. And if a state doesn't sell to 18-year-olds, a bordering state often does.

[12] • Parental approval. Most parents feel a sense of relief when their children turn to booze rather than to marijuana or heroin. Compared to tales they've heard about drug abuse—wasted minds, changed personalities, suicides, insanity—the dangers of a little alcohol hardly seem much to get excited about.

[13] As a result of such attitudes, many teens drink with parental approval. Some parents even encourage their teenagers to drink with them in the home. "We would rather have Sally drink with us where we know she's safe," one father was quoted as saying, "than behind our backs."

[14] What is the answer to the problem? Does the answer lie in the schools and in teaching the dangers of alcohol and other drugs? Or is it a matter of reeducating the entire population, adults and young people alike? Dr. Morris Chafetz, director of the National Institute on Alcohol and Alcohol Abuse, has this answer: "People in America are never going to come to grips with the drug problems of young people until they take a long, hard look at how they use, and misuse, alcohol themselves."

I NEVER HAD IT MADE

Jackie Robinson

[1] I guess if I could choose one of the most important moments in my life, I would go back to 1947, in the Yankee Stadium in New York City. It was the opening day of the world series and I was for the first time playing in the series as a member of the Brooklyn Dodgers team. It was a history-making day. It would be the first time that a black man would be allowed to participate in a world series. I had become the first black player in the major leagues.

[2] I was proud of that and yet I was uneasy. I was proud to be in the hurricane eye of a significant breakthrough and to be used to prove that a sport can't be called national if blacks are barred from it. Branch Rickey, the president of the Brooklyn Dodgers, had rudely awakened America. He was a man with high ideals, and he was also a shrewd businessman. Mr. Rickey had shocked some of his fellow baseball tycoons and angered others by deciding to smash the unwritten law that kept blacks out of the big leagues. He had chosen me as the person to lead the way.

[3] It hadn't been easy. Some of my own teammates refused to accept me because I was black. I had been forced to live with snubs and rebuffs and rejections. Within the club, Mr. Rickey had put down rebellion by letting my teammates know that anyone who didn't want to accept me could leave. But the problems within the Dodgers club had been minor compared to the opposition outside. It hadn't been that easy to fight the resentment expressed by players on other teams, by the team owners, or by bigoted fans screaming "nigger." The hate mail piled up. There were threats against me and my family and even out-and-out attempts at physical harm to me.

[4] Some things counterbalanced this ugliness. Black people supported me with total loyalty. They supported me morally; they came to sit in a hostile audience in unprecedented numbers to make the turnstiles hum as they never had before at ball parks all over the nation. Money is America's God, and business people can dig black power if it coincides with green power, so these fans were important to the success of Mr. Rickey's "Noble Experiment."

[5] Some of the Dodgers who swore they would never play with a black man had a change of mind, when they realized I was a good ball player who could be helpful in their earning a few thousand more dollars in world series money. After the initial resistance to me had been crushed, my teammates started to give me tips on how to improve my game. They

hadn't changed because they liked me any better; they had changed because I could help fill their wallets.

[6] My fellow Dodgers were not decent out of self-interest alone. There were heartwarming experiences with some teammates; there was Southern-born Pee Wee Reese who turned into a staunch friend. And there were others.

[7] Mr. Rickey stands out as the man who inspired me the most. He will always have my admiration and respect. Critics had said, "Don't you know that your precious Mr. Rickey didn't bring you up out of the black leagues because he loved you? Are you stupid enough not to understand that the Brooklyn club profited hugely because of what your Mr. Rickey did?"

[8] Yes, I know that. But I also know what a big gamble he took. A bond developed between us that lasted long after I had left the game. In a way I feel I was the son he had lost and he was the father I had lost.

[9] There was more than just making money at stake in Mr. Rickey's decision. I learned that his family was afraid that his health was being undermined by the resulting pressures and that they pleaded with him to abandon the plan. His peers and fellow baseball moguls exerted all kinds of influence to get him to change his mind. Some of the press condemned him as a fool and a demagogue. But he didn't give in.

[10] In a very real sense, black people helped make the experiment succeed. Many who came to the ball park had not been baseball fans before I began to play in the big leagues. Suppressed and repressed for so many years, they needed a victorious black man as a symbol. It would help them believe in themselves. But black support of the first black man in the majors was a complicated matter. The breakthrough created as much danger as it did hope. It was one thing for me out there on the playing field to be able to keep my cool in the face of insults. But it was another for all those black people sitting in the stands to keep from overreacting when they sensed a racial slur or an unjust decision. They could have blown the whole bit to hell by acting belligerently and touching off a race riot. That would have been all the bigots needed to set back the cause of progress of black men in sports another hundred years. I knew this. Mr. Rickey knew this. But this never happened. I learned from Rachel who had spent hours in the stands that clergymen and laymen had held meetings in the black community to spread the word. We all knew about the help of the black press. Mr. Rickey and I owed them a great deal.

[11] Children from all races came to the stands. The very young seemed to have no hangup at all about my being black. They just wanted me to be good, to deliver, to win. The inspiration of their innocence is amazing. I don't think I'll ever forget the small, shrill voice of a tiny white kid who, in the midst of a racially tense atmosphere during an early game in a Dixie town, cried out, "Attaboy, Jackie." It broke the tension and it made me feel I had to succeed.

[12] The black and the young were my cheering squads. But also there were people—neither black nor young—people of all races and faiths and in all parts of this country, people who couldn't care less about my race.

[13] Rachel was even more important to my success. I know that every successful man is supposed to say that without his wife he could never have accomplished success. It is gospel in my case. Rachel shared those difficult years that led to this moment and helped me through all the days thereafter. She has been strong, loving, gentle, and brave, never afraid to either criticize or comfort me.

[14] There I was the black grandson of a slave, the son of a black sharecropper, part of a historic occasion, a symbolic hero to my people. The air was sparkling. The sunlight was warm. The band struck up the national anthem. The flag billowed in the wind. It should have been a glorious moment for me as the stirring words of the national anthem poured from the stands. Perhaps it was, but then again perhaps the anthem could be called the theme song for a drama called *The Noble Experiment*. Today as I look back on that opening game of my first world series, I must tell you that it was Mr. Rickey's drama and that I was only a principal actor. As I write this twenty years later, I cannot stand and sing the anthem. I cannot salute the flag; I know that I am a black man in a white world. In 1972, in 1947, at my birth in 1919, I know that I never had it made.

UFOs
Isaac Asimov

[1] When most people think about flying saucers or, as they are more austerely called, "unidentified flying objects" (UFOs), they think of them as spaceships coming from outside Earth, and manned by intelligent beings.

[2] Is there any chance of this? Do the "little green men" really exist? There are arguments pro and con.

[3] *Pro.* There is, according to the best astronomical thinking today, a strong chance that life is very common in the universe. Our own galaxy, containing over a hundred billion stars, is only one of perhaps a hundred billion galaxies.

[4] Current theories about how stars are formed make it seem likely that planets are formed also, so that every star may have planets about it. Surely *some* of those planets would be like our Earth in chemistry and temperature.

[5] Current theories about how life got its start make it seem that any planet with something like Earth's chemistry and temperature would be sure to develop life. One reasonable estimate advanced by an astronomer was that there might be as many as 640,000,000 planets in our galaxy alone that are Earthlike and that bear life.

[6] But on how many of these planets is there *intelligent* life? We can't say, but suppose that only one out of a million life-bearing planets develops intelligent life forms and that only one out of ten of these develops a technological civilization more advanced than our own. There might still be as many as 100 different advanced civilizations in our galaxy, and perhaps a hundred more in every other galaxy. Why shouldn't some of them have reached us?

[7] *Con.* Assuming there are 100 advanced civilizations in our own galaxy and that they are evenly spread throughout the galaxy, the nearest one would be about 10,000 light-years away. Even assuming coverage of that distance at the fastest speed we know of—the speed of light—the trip would take at least 10,000 years. Why should anyone make such long journeys just to poke around curiously?

[8] *Pro.* It is wrong to try to estimate the abilities of a far-advanced civilization, or their motives either. For one thing, the situation may not be average. The nearest advanced civilization may just happen to be only 100 light-years away, rather than 10,000.

[9] Furthermore, because *we* know of no practical way of traveling faster than light doesn't mean an advanced civilization may not know of

one. To an advanced civilization a distance of 100 light-years or even 10,000 light-years may be very little. They may be delighted to explore over long distances just for the sake of exploring.

[10] *Con.* But even if that were the case, it would make no sense to send so many spaceships so often (judging by the many UFO reports). Surely we are not *that* interesting. And if we *are* interesting, why not land and greet us? Or communicate without landing? They can't be afraid of us, since if they are so far advanced beyond us, they can surely defend themselves against any puny threats we can offer.

[11] On the other hand, if they want to be merely observers, and not interfere with the development of our civilization in any way, they could surely so handle their observations that we would not be continually aware of them.

[12] *Pro.* Again, we can't try to guess what the motives of these explorers might be. What might seem logical to us, might not seem so logical to them. They may not care if we see them, and they also may not care to say hello. Besides, there are many reports of people who have seen the ships and have even been aboard. Surely some of these reports must have something to them.

[13] *Con.* Eyewitness reports of actual spaceships and actual extraterrestrials are, in themselves, totally unreliable. There have been innumerable eyewitness reports of almost everything that most rational people do not care to accept—of ghosts, angels, levitation, zombies, werewolves, and so on.

[14] What we really want, in this case, is something *material;* some object or artifact that is clearly not of human manufacture or Earthly origin. These people who claim to have seen or entered a spaceship never end up with any button, rag, or other *object* that would substantiate their story.

[15] *Pro.* But how else can you account for all the UFO reports? Even after you exclude the mistaken, the gags and hoaxes—there remain many sightings that can't be explained by scientists within the present limits of knowledge. Aren't we forced to suppose these sightings are extraterrestrial spaceships?

[16] *Con.* No, because we don't know that the extraterrestrial spaceship is the *only* remaining explanation. If we can't think of any other, that may simply be a defect in our imagination. If an answer is unknown, then it is simply unknown. An Unidentified Flying Object is just that—unidentified.

[17] The most serious and levelheaded investigator of UFOs I know is J. Allen Hynek, a logical astronomer who is convinced that some UFO reports are worth serious investigation. He doesn't think they represent extraterrestrial spaceships, but he does suggest that they represent phenomena that lie outside the present structure of science, and that understanding them will help us expand our knowledge and build a greatly enlarged structure of science.

[18] The trouble is that whatever the UFO phenomenon is, it comes and goes unexpectedly. There is no way of examining it systematically. It appears suddenly and accidentally, is partially seen, and then is more or less inaccurately reported. We remain dependent on occasional anecdotal accounts.

[19] Dr. Hynek, after a quarter of a century of devoted and honest research, so far ends with nothing. He not only has no solution, but he has no real idea of any possible solution. He has only his belief that when the solution comes it will be important.

[20] He may be right, but there are at least equal grounds for believing that the solution may never come, or that when it comes, it will be unimportant.